PSYCHOANALYSIS AND SOCIAL RESEARCH

Psychoanalysis and Social Research

THE PSYCHOANALYTIC STUDY
OF THE NON-PATIENT

Herbert Hendin, M.D.

Willard Gaylin, M.D.

Arthur Carr, Ph.D.

DOUBLEDAY & COMPANY, INC.

GARDEN CITY, NEW YORK

1965

This study was made possible by a grant from
the National Institute of Mental Health (MH 07207–01).

Contents

PSYCHOANALYSIS AND SOCIAL RESEARCH

Introduction

Four major disciplines—sociology, anthropology, psychology, and psychiatry—are actively engaged in the study of psychosocial problems ranging from sex to suicide. Yet despite this multiplicity of effort, psychosocial research, that is, research into problems that are both psychological and sociological in nature, has suffered under a fundamental handicap in trying to obtain essential facts.

The information elicited by the usual interviewing procedures, even when conducted by trained observers, is of limited value and can be misleading. The answers to questions usually reflect what the subject wants to feel, thinks he feels, or thinks he is expected to feel. As psychoanalysis has demonstrated, individuals are not consciously aware of most of the significant attitudes and dynamic patterns shaping their thinking and behavior.

The psychoanalytic interview, based on free associations, unconscious reactions, dreams, and fantasies, is capable of exposing both conscious and unconscious factors, desires and

1

defenses—and the individual often reveals his inner feelings unawares. The difference between the conventional and the psychoanalytic approach to obtaining information was dramatized for one of the authors in a psychosocial study he recently completed in Scandinavia.[1] In a sociological survey of Norway published in 1955, David Rodnick accepted at face value statements by Norwegian women that in their country the woman plays a completely submissive role in marriage.[2] Hendin, on the other hand, found that when Norwegian women holding this opinion began to talk freely about their own lives, the trend of their associations indicated something quite different; they unwittingly revealed that they considered themselves stronger than their husbands, that their mothers dominated their fathers, and that the woman was the more effective figure in most of their friends' marriages. They dreamed of their men as babies or children. If pressed about the contradiction, they usually admitted that "women are stronger than men, but a man must be allowed to think he is stronger."

What people consider they should feel is indicative of certain social values in the culture. When asked if she were a good nurse, not one of twelve Norwegian nurses would say yes. "I'm average," or "My superiors think I'm all right," were the usual replies. To the same question, eleven out of twelve American girls did reply yes. This does not indicate a greater self-confidence on the part of American nurses; it rather reflects the Norwegian cultural attitude that one simply does not say one is good at something and the contrasting American attitude that one must project a belief in one's own competence if others are to believe in it. Social attitudes like this are not difficult to ascertain, but unconscious attitudes —visualizing men as children—can be determined only through free associations, dreams, and fantasies.

The mass of social research that relies primarily upon statistical data avoids such problems. Relatively accurate information can be obtained about birth, marriage, and divorce rates, although the problem is somewhat more complicated when the rates for suicide, homicide, and chronic alcoholism

[1] Herbert Hendin, *Suicide and Scandinavia,* Doubleday Anchor, 1965.
[2] David Rodnick, *The Norwegians,* Public Affairs Press, 1955.

2

are to be determined. In many situations it is hard to decide if a death is due to homicide, suicide, or accident. The usually given and relatively accurate figures for the national yearly consumption of alcohol tell us nothing of the incidence of problem drinking.

In some areas where statistics are not available, we have needed efforts like the Kinsey report,[3] to fill the gap. When Kinsey asked questions such as those aimed at establishing the incidence of premarital sexual experience among women he was, despite the personal nature of the questions, on relatively safe ground. With the notable exception of his inquiries about female orgasm, his subjects at least knew the answers to his questions so that he had to be concerned only with their truthfulness.

However, Kinsey's interest was behavior, not motivation, and part of his focus on behavior was admittedly an attempt to avoid having to deal with motives. He was not concerned with the subject's reasons for having sexual experience or the emotions that accompanied the experience. This was his prerogative, although from a psychoanalytic standpoint there is a crucial difference between a girl desiring sex with a boy or merely fearing to lose him if she withholds consent, and Kinsey's failure to make such distinctions tends to invalidate many of his conclusions and recommendations. For example, because his figures show a relatively high incidence of male homosexuality, Kinsey concluded that homosexuality is not a neurotic variation of sexual behavior. The present authors, in common with others who have done psychoanalytic studies of male homosexuality, have on the other hand been impressed by the destuctive and neurotic motivations that invariably characterize homosexual relationships, whether or not the homosexual seeks help.[4] Kinsey's conclusion could come only from an exclusive concentration on what people do rather than how they feel.

Research in the social sciences that is far more sophisticated than the Kinsey report runs into similar difficulties. Descrip-

[3] Alfred Kinsey, Wardell Pomeroy, and Clyde Martin, *Sexual Behavior in the Human Male*, W. B. Saunders, 1945. *Sexual Behavior in the Human Female*, W. B. Saunders, 1953.
[4] Lionel Ovesey, Willard Gaylin, and Herbert Hendin, "Psychotherapy of Male Homosexuality," *Archives of General Psychiatry* IX pp. 19–31, July 1963.

tions of social institutions and social behavior based on their characteristic patterns have given us such provocative designations as "the other-directed man"[5] and "the organization man."[6] Social character is the popular term in social science for describing such patterns of social behavior. Character, however, refers to what one is—feelings and motives included —and not merely to observable behavior. It is one thing to describe social institutions and social behavior; to understand them fully one must be able to grasp their effect on the individual. This requires a more sensitive instrument than has been available in psychosocial research.

Psychoanalysis would seem to be such an instrument. In his daily work with patients, the psychoanalyst elicits feelings and motives, the unconscious as well as the conscious, the unexpressed as well as the expressed. Yet the very word "patient" suggests another side to the problem. Has experience with patients any validity with a non-patient population where, presumably, the pain of sickness and the desire for help, which lead a patient to expose himself, do not exist?

The same question of patient versus non-patient arises in utilizing psychological tests such as the Rorschach (ink blot) and the Thematic Apperception Test (pictures of people and situations). Developed primarily with clinical populations, the interpretation of such tests is enhanced by the therapist's overall clinical knowledge of the patient. When such knowledge is not available, as in the industrial use of tests with non-patients, frequent errors in the estimation of the subject's adaptive capacities result. When such testing has ignored motivation and concentrated on attitudes and preferences as elicited by questionnaire, the errors have been even greater. While the Rorschach and Thematic Apperception Test (TAT) are revealing of the motivational aspects of behavior, the prediction of overt behavior from them has been shown to be most difficult.[7, 8] Lacking the equivalent of the clinical

[5] David Riesman, Reuel Denney, and Nathan Glazer, *The Lonely Crowd,* Yale University Press, 1950.
[6] William H. Whyte, Jr., *The Organization Man,* Doubleday Anchor, 1957.
[7] Evelyn Hooker, "Male Homosexuality in the Rorschach," *J. Projective Tech.,* 21:18–31, 1957.
[8] Arthur Carr et al., *The Prediction of Overt Behavior Through the Use of Projective Techniques.* Charles C. Thomas, 1960.

information available about patients, psychological tests have fallen short of being an ideal method for the study of social problems.

In the recently developing attempts to apply psychoanalysis to the study of social problems, the psychoanalyst usually works on the premise that patients are a barometer of the pressures existing on all people in the society, whether or not they need or seek help. The natural outgrowth of the desire to test this premise is the study of non-patients. In his Scandinavian work, Hendin had the opportunity of utilizing psychoanalytic interviews with both patients and non-patients. The predominant psychological characteristics seen in Norwegian patients differed from those of Swedish patients, but the patterns observed in both groups correlated well with those observed in Norwegians and Swedes who were non-patients.

To take but one example, complaints of emotional constriction, apathy, and even deadness were common among Swedish patients and non-patients alike, but were rarely mentioned by Norwegians in either group. The patients in both countries seemed to serve as an exaggerated mirror for viewing the psychosocial problems of their society, suggesting that valuable results might be obtained by utilizing both patients and non-patients in psychosocial research and emphasizing the importance of studying further the possibilities of psychoanalytic interviews with non-patients.

In the course of the previously mentioned research project exploring the nature of male homosexuality, the authors were further impressed by the importance of analytically surveying a non-patient population. Culturally determined attitudes about success and failure, strength and weakness, power and vulnerability, and their relationship to masculinity and femininity, play a significant role in the formation of the homosexual symptom. These cultural attitudes and their sources must be studied directly with non-patient populations to determine their presence or absence and the ways in which the "normal" individual manages to integrate these forces into a successful adaptation.

The possibilities are exciting. If the use of psychoanalytic interviewing techniques proves feasible in the study of non-patients, it will provide an important independent instrument for studying the individual and his society, and will open up vast new possibilities for psychosocial research.

The present research study was designed as a pilot project to test to what degree a psychoanalytic approach would be useful in the psychosocial exploration of non-patient populations. Nurses were selected as the test group purely from the standpoint of convenience and availability. There was no intention to draw conclusions from the study about nurses as a group or to determine the personality factors that might lead a girl to choose this profession, although, as mentioned in the conclusion, the results did open up some interesting future possibilities along these lines. But the primary purpose of this study was to see what information the use of psychoanalytic techniques would provide with a sampling of non-patients chosen to some extent at random.

Since asking for volunteers would obviously have been self-defeating, the following procedure was followed: A hospital was selected where the investigators were not known. Forty nurses, the entire day roster, exclusive of psychiatric nurses, were approached. In a most general and non-specific way, they were told that only twelve of their group were being asked to participate in the research, but that since a random sampling was needed, it was hoped that all would agree to co-operate. All did agree to participate, if chosen. Twelve nurses were then selected by lot.

They were each seen for a total of five hours, an hour at a time, on a twice-a-week basis. Each nurse's interviews were completed within three weeks. Spacing of the sessions was based on the desire to achieve continuity from session to session and yet allow enough time for development of the subject's emotional reactions to the interviewing and the interviewer. It is a psychoanalytic cliché that the patient often exposes his significant psychodynamic constellations in the first few hours—that even the core of the neurosis may be represented in the first dream brought by the patient to the analyst. Based on this observation and experience with non-patients in Scandinavia, it was hoped that five sessions would prove adequate.

Limiting the number of sessions also served the purpose of restricting the subject's own awareness of the problems she was revealing. Such awareness without continuing therapeutic help is, of course, apt to be disturbing. The first girl to be

6

discussed, for example, reveals through her dreams and associations a disappointment with her fiancé (and men in general) that is at complete variance with her consciously stated attitudes. She has, however, made an adequate adaptation, and it would be a disservice to make her aware of this contradiction.

Since the nurses had to come for the interviews on their own time and often on their day off, they were paid $25.00 for completing the five sessions. The possibility of giving them time off from their working day and paying the hospital to substitute for them was considered, but it was administratively much simpler for the hospital not to have to be concerned with such a procedure.

Each nurse was also given a standard battery of psychological tests. The psychologist conducting testing worked completely apart from the interviewers, however, and prepared an independent evaluation of each nurse.

The presentation of the case histories raised certain problems. Since the research is essentially methodological, the major interest is in the interview rather than the subject. The interviews were recorded as nearly verbatim as possible. Since presenting sixty hours of interviews in this fashion is obviously impractical, it was decided that one case should be so presented to give an idea of the style and flow of the interviews. Case I was selected for this purpose. It will be seen that she is not the sickest, or most dramatic, but represents what may be an approximation of the typical interview.

Cases II to VIII are presented in various degrees of condensation in an attempt to achieve economy of space while still, hopefully, retaining the spirit and special problems of the interviews. Cases IX to XII would have added little more to an understanding of our method. They are therefore being presented briefly merely to illuminate specific unique points of view. In all cases minor factual changes have been made in such matters as names and places so as to conceal the identity of the individual without compromising the integrity of the material.

CASE I

(Miss A)

Miss A was twenty-two, of medium height with average looks and a somewhat serious facial expression. Her dress and manner had an indifferent quality that did little to enhance her femininity. She was informed, as were all the subjects at the beginning of the first interview, that the interviewer wished to get as complete a picture of her as possible, and that it would be best if she told about herself in her own way.

First Interview

How many people are you seeing? (Twelve.) I wonder how much can be learned from so small a number. [Thirty seconds silence.]

I feel on the spot. Is there anything special you wish to know? (Everything.) I come from Newark. Spent all my life there. My father is a doctor. [Twenty seconds silence.] It's not that my life is a blank, it's just hard. I have a brother who

9

is sixteen. I suppose you want to know about him. He seemed no different in school, but he took criticism to heart. It's hard for him to keep his head above the water. He had to go to a private high school. [She smiled often, quite nervously.]

Since I recall, I wanted to do nothing else but nursing. To my teachers, nursing was not an honorable or admirable profession. There were some stumbling blocks there. I was considering going on the five-year plan, but I felt something might happen to interrupt things and I'd be nowhere. (Happen?) If I had to drop out or didn't care for it. I know now I could have changed my mind. I asked my parents if Dad being a doctor influenced me in any way. I wasn't part of his medical life. In a medical family there is more discussion, and my questions are answered. At this point I'm undecided about going on. Right now I'm satisfied. I'm getting married in January. My husband will be in school. I'm not sure if I'll go back to school or not. [Twenty seconds silence.]

Well, my brother, he developed as a boy all right, but then he went to school and he had difficulty with reading. He was ushered off to this and that psychiatrist. He was bright in every other respect. My parents changed him to a private school. He progressed fairly well. He had tutors in the home. They were considering that he should be left back. Then they found a place, a special school, for him in Connecticut, a boys' school. It's small. He is sixteen now. He's still lagging behind in certain respects. (Just what sort of difficulty does your brother have?) Well, it started the time he was six and I was eleven. They told my mother that it was my mother's fault, that she was overbearing. I can't see my mother that way. I'd like to know what triggered it off. By the time he was twelve he was sent off to this school. [Her early emphasis on her brother's difficulties was noteworthy, and it appeared hard for her to go into more detail about him. Since it was early in her first session, she was not pressed any further to do so.]

I was always closer to my mother than my father. I've been thinking about this, not in connection with coming here. I thought about it in training. Not that I loved my mother more than him. He and I have the same disposition. The same things irritate us. He's not easy to talk with. I always needed one confidante. My mother is my confidante. She knows everything with regard to me. My father is difficult to talk to, for others too. Professionally I have no way of knowing. My mother is quiet. My father is not bombastic, but he has moments of anger when he will speak out. Mother is more easygoing. She's highly nervous but doesn't show it as much. I'm skipping around a lot. Is it O.K. to smoke? (Sure.) My parents told me they had been proud of me. I got into no real trouble. My father shows it. He talks to others as though his daughter has conquered the world. He gets carried overboard.

My father's mother died when I was eleven. She had Huntington's chorea,[1] the hereditary one. There were four sisters and two brothers, and three sisters and the two brothers had it. My grandfather was a domineering man. He ruled the family with an iron fist. My grandmother had symptoms. He made her play the part of an invalid. My grandfather saw to the cooking. He was penurious. He wouldn't permit my grandmother to have any money. He wouldn't let her shop herself. She was subservient. My mother tells how when they were first married they lived in the same building with my grandparents. My grandfather tried hard to govern my mother and father's marriage in the beginning. My grandfather is living in Vermont, so I see him very infrequently. I really don't know him, only through my parents. He used to check on all that my parents did. He wished all to go right. He has never shown any affection for anyone. He's a very odd type of person. My parents then moved, but only blocks away. We stayed there. However, my grandparents moved away to Vermont when I was six. When I used to go to their house before I was six, he was not in evidence. I do recall affection from my grandmother. He never kissed me even as a child. Now it's a funny period. I went up there last summer. They didn't ask me about my engagement. (Didn't you tell them?) He didn't ask. [She appeared to be indicating here that the interviewer would also have to ask, and this turned out to be the case.]

He's bitter. Nothing is good. Like a gossipy little old woman. He had a wife and raised two boys. [She appeared angry in discussing this.] He cooks and shops. She wasn't really so helpless. Since I know him, and it's not just my opinion, but the whole family's, he's a bitter person. My father

[1] Huntington's chorea—a hereditary affliction of adults marked by irregular movements, speech disturbances, and dementia.

11

tells how there were no Christmas celebrations. He takes no interest in anything unless it's something bad. If I were marrying a Hindu, maybe. He said to my aunt, 'All that school and now she's getting married?' My father turned out very generous to a fault. He doesn't want us to need everything. [Her voice was at times anxious, at times had a hissing quality.] It seems off the subject, all this with regard to my grandfather. (Are you surprised to find yourself discussing him?) Well, we discussed him at home recently. My uncle and father have some of the same traits. My uncle was no success. My father had a successful career. My aunt discussed how my grandfather influenced him. My father and uncle are both not demonstrative like my grandfather. My mother is more demonstrative. My father has no pet names for the children. He doesn't take an active part with my brother and myself. He seems embarrassed to show affection. My mother kisses me with ease. My father is ill at ease kissing us. It is natural considering my grandfather never kissed anyone. [She threw up her hands in saying this.] My uncle and father are not close.

My mother's parents died. My mother's father when she was six, my mother's mother when she was thirteen. Mother was put into girls' boarding school which to my knowledge she enjoyed. She was not close to her family. She had cousins and a half sister. She went to business school after that. She worked in school.

Is there something special you want me to discuss? There doesn't seem to be anything like that with me. [Her reaction to the interviewer seemed to have stimulated her into revealing feelings toward her grandfather, her father, and men in general. However, it seemed that she had now begun using biographical data about her family as a way of avoiding talking about herself. The interviewer felt it might be helpful to call this to her attention and it should be noted that a rather striking trend of associations followed.]

(Is it easier to talk about your grandfather and mother than about yourself?) I don't know what to tell you about me. There isn't much to discuss about myself. I'm not as interesting. It doesn't come as easy. I recall little things. I recall starting school, what I wore in kindergarten. I recall things that frightened me. I was shy. I was horrified. The teachers looked in your hair, in your ears, and at my underwear. I was

modest. It wasn't their business. They were weird people. I
can't draw to this day. It started in kindergarten. I was never
allowed to paint at the easels. I could never think of anything
to paint. I drew a bus. My first-grade teacher told me it was
more like a garbage truck. Then all I drew was painful. If
Miss Z [the psychologist] saw the pictures I drew for her,
she would have thought I hated men. They were so very odd.
I was sensitive. I was good. I didn't do anything wrong. The
teacher reprimanded the class, I took it as a personal insult.
I still am sensitive. If you were to say something about something I say, I'd mull over it. I'm more conscious of people
looking at me than anyone I know. I'm self-conscious. I don't
want anyone to notice me. Now I realize people are not always
looking. As a little girl I was conscious. I wouldn't get up on
stage. And I felt that was wrong, and I did get up. Yet I'd be
half sick to my stomach. I'd go into a decline two days before. In class I liked to sing but I feared to sing alone. As far
as work went, I didn't fear questions if I knew the answer. I
recall situations where I had to do it alone, things in school.
Do you want me to go into that? (Yes, if that's on your
mind.) The oddest thing, in the first grade, the teacher was
odd. She had taught my father and uncle. I was eager to go to
school. We had new tables. I don't recall the first grade other
than the pupils. The only bad memory is the picture that
looked like a garbage truck. I recall going to be registered. I
recall the girl going down on the slide. I recall the boy who
moved his bowels in his pants every day at the same time.
We all knew who it was. The teacher always acted like it was
the first time it happened. We had to check and find out.
[END OF FIRST SESSION.]

In summary, it should be noted that she begins the session
by discussing her brother and his emotional difficulties, particularly with her mother. She makes clear that she has han-
dled her mother by being an obedient daughter and has been
close to her mother as a consequence. The trend of her associations—going from her brother's difficulties to her own
obedient adjustment and then to the theme of hereditary illness in her mother's family—arouses at least the suspicion that
she fears becoming emotionally disturbed if she does not
avoid her brother's course of action with her mother.

In going on to discuss her grandparents she appears to reveal a good deal about her own family, as well as her reac-

13

tion to the interviewer. Her sympathy and loyalty are with her grandmother and her mother. She speaks of her grandfather as unemotional, aloof, and indifferent to her, and indicates her father also has these qualities, although it is evidently safer to make the indictment of her grandfather. In addition, the theme of emotional aloofness and indifference appear related to the interviewer's not asking questions and the anxiety this is generating. This anxiety was allowed to continue since she appeared able to handle it, and it was proving to be productive.

The seemingly gentle question as to whether it was easier to talk about her grandfather than about herself was evidently perceived as quite threatening and produced a good deal of paranoid imagery involving having her ears, hair, and underwear examined and culminating in her memory of the child who soiled himself in school. She appeared quite capable, however, of handling this increased anxiety.

Second Interview

How are you? (Fine, thank you. How are you?) O.K. Well, I'll start with school. I had a close friend through high school. The only trouble was that she was dominant. When I got to be about ten, I began feeling my own strength, and we were not so close any more. Now in training, she has her own circle and I have mine. [Twenty seconds of silence.] I had my tonsils out in the second grade in Newark. [Thirty seconds silence.]

How detailed should I be? [Thirty seconds silence.] In the eighth grade I had a close circle of friends. My parents suggested I should go to private school. I was very much against it. I never had had to meet new friends. I went to this school for a week, and I was happy to be there. For a time I kept in touch, then I began to make new friends. In high school, the high school was small, and I overcame my shyness. I took part in all the activities, and I became vice president of my class. I did well in high school. I was interested in the work.

Training was hard in the beginning. It was a struggle for the first six months, but I've been a good student. All the girls—some were very bright, and some were mediocre—but all of them wanted to be a nurse so badly. I went to see a

14

guidance counselor. She allayed my fears. Time passed, and I found my own level. The second and third years my marks improved, and I was quite sure of myself. In the beginning I felt the instructors were cold, that I couldn't talk to them. A lot of girls felt the same. Later I realized it was done for a purpose. (Purpose?) You have to learn to stand on your own two feet. It's been explained. I felt a soft word now and then, and I would have been fine.

I wanted to be a psychiatric nurse. I was told it was an odd thing to do, that you must see all first. I was always interested in people's problems. When we went to C [her psychiatric affiliation], I didn't like it at all. I enjoyed the theory. (What didn't you like?) Well, I was on the male unit. I didn't understand much. There were young boys not much older than me. I wasn't attached to anyone. One boy of sixteen, he got to talk to me. They were wavering in the diagnosis between psychopathic personality or inadequate personality. He got attached to me. It would have been the same with any young girl there. I felt all he needed was a good talking to. I realized better later. Then on the female section I didn't like the head nurse. She frightened me. I hate physical violence. Someone acting up and you have to restrain them with packs and baths. I got depressed after two weeks there. I was afraid to go to work. I had gone with an open mind, with the feeling that this exists. I wasn't the first one there. But I couldn't accept it. I told the woman there I can't contribute if I'm miserable. They thought it would be all right because I was good in theory. On the convalescent floor my interest waned. I was interested in theory. I felt inadequate to deal with psychological problems. All the bizarre behavior there. I went there without any great fear. In high school I had gotten interested in Freud. I plowed through the books available in pocketbook form. It wasn't soul-searching. I wasn't comparing it with myself. But there I was frightened. The head nurse made me do things we were taught not to do. One woman was hallucinating. I was told to take her temperature rectally. [Her voice quivered at this point.] The nurse told me to take her temperature. The patient would have no part of it. She was agitated. She was in a seclusion room. The nurse then told me to go back and try again. The woman pushed me out of the room and she made me go back a third time. I said, "Lie down!" She grabbed my hand and broke the thermometer. I tussled with her and I got half of it away from her. I went back to the nurse's desk. I was shaking. The head nurse grabbed me by the nape of the neck, and she went in. As soon as she came in, the patient lay down quietly. Things had started out without trouble. With tube feeding I felt frightened a little. I felt the place was cruel. But she had a lot to do with my fear. Maybe not. I can't put my finger on the reason. I found it easy to be attached, talk, form a bond. They would talk to me alone. It wasn't me. It would be anyone who listened. I know it's not for me, this field, unless I know and can overcome my problems with it. I felt the field was a baby, had a long way to go. Perhaps someone could change my opinions, but I feel it has a long way to go. Are you a psychiatrist? (Yes, I am.)

[Throughout the above sequence the subject continued with the memories of fear and violence that had characterized the last half of her first hour. The interviewer had the feeling that a good deal of this dread was in response to the anxiety stirred up by the first session. Her going from this trend to the question, Are you a psychiatrist? seemed to offer some confirmation of this idea.]

It would be interesting to hear your opinion about what I say. You probably feel different. We don't really get training in psychiatry. I never felt more normal than up here. I know I have certain weaknesses, some personality traits that would flare up if I were sick. (What do you consider your weaknesses?) Up there I tried to put myself in the schizophrenic category. I'm an introverted character, I believe. I'm more of an introvert than an extrovert. But I like people, yet I enjoy being alone. I like to read, not sit and just think. Schizophrenics are more arty. I'm not. They're more compulsive soul-searchers. (Just what do you mean by "weaknesses?") I have mood swings. I tend to cry easily. Sadness and happiness alike can make me cry. I'm happy, my eyes fill up. I'm sad, I feel a great relief in crying. I watch a movie and cry. I see a person on the street and I feel sorry for them. I feel I have it so good and others have it hard. Not for position in life, more for infirmities or burdens they have to bear. I get angry at times and I think I have paranoid tendencies. Maybe I shouldn't tell you. Especially when I'm depressed. I think maybe they think I don't do a good job. It follows what I felt when younger. It doesn't disturb me. I wish to get over my insecurity in training. I overcame my skitterishness about opening my mouth. In high school I followed the group. There was a period when I didn't wish to be different. I didn't go through a giddy and silly stage. I wished to be serious and given responsibility. [She moves her body a good deal in talking, frequently scratches her nose.] I was close to my Latin teacher, who had a son in my class. She had a schizophrenic daughter. She was interested in my going to college. She wrote to the school that I should do the college plan. When I went into training, our friendship dwindled. She felt I was running around with a mop in my hand.

[Since she had brought up the subject of nursing the interviewer used the occasion to ask her several questions about her attitude toward nursing as a profession. As will be seen, the remainder of the interview is directed toward getting factual information or toward encouraging her to report her dreams.]

(Why did you decide to go into training?) I can't recall when I decided. I wished to find out. My parents agreed that I should find out if I liked it, and I was an aide over the summer. I like people, I like talking to them. I wished to help in some way. (If you had to do it over, would you become a nurse?) I couldn't say. I'm sure I would. I didn't enjoy the first year. I'd like to change a lot. (What would you like to change?) Oh, please! We don't have time for the patients. We're doing dishes and clerical work and cleaning, not dealing with people. (Do you feel you're a good nurse?) Yes, because I'm interested, and many are not. I have a lot to learn. I know very little. The thing that little girls dream of as far as nursing has changed a good deal. But there's enjoyment in seeing the response of the patients in making someone comfortable. Not all nurses feel this way, believe me, especially around here. (What do you feel your weaknesses are as a nurse?) Oh, they're not unusual. I get irritated at times. I'm compulsive. It's impossible to be satisfied with compulsivity in a hospital. I'm not easygoing about responsibility.

(Have you had any dreams lately?) No. (Do you recall any of your past dreams?) I had one recurrent dream in childhood about heaven. I crossed over a bridge and went into a church. There was velvet carpeting. No people were in there. I saw Jesus there. It was a pleasant dream which re-

17

curred when I was six, seven, or eight, very frequently. (What is your religious background?) I'm Presbyterian. There was a period in high school I doubted all organized religion. (Are your parents religious?) My mother is Episcopal. They both go to church. (Do you believe in God?) Oh yes. (Afterlife?) Yes, I believe in heaven. (Do you think all go there?) Well, I haven't thought. In my own mind, I can understand immortality. I don't believe you're punished in an afterlife. [END OF SESSION.]

The subject began the second interview as she had the first, by asking a question. Through her discussion early in the session of the way she was directed in training, i.e., purposely without encouragement, she got across her need for more encouragement and responsiveness from the interviewer. She did not get it, and her associations—whether dealing with the removal of her tonsils or her experiences in the psychiatric hospital—then became marked by imagery suggesting violation of the bodily integrity of one individual by another.

Third Interview

I'm sorry I'm late. [She had been one or two minutes late.] I don't know what you are interested in hearing about. (You haven't told me about your boy friend and your forthcoming marriage.) [She was pleased at being asked and was quite willing to talk about it.] I'm marrying a boy that I knew since childhood, since I was five years old. I'd see him each summer at a summer place. I didn't consider him my boy friend when I grew up. He went into the Army at eighteen. We started dating. Suddenly we discussed that this was it. That was two and a half years ago. It will be three years that we're engaged last May. He is going to New York University. He's getting an accounting degree with a minor in law. He had to change to night school. He is putting himself through. He's twenty-three. He'll be twenty-four in August. He's a quiet type of person, which I like. I'm not the uproarious type. We enjoy the same things. Our goals are the same. We both like children. We don't plan a family till he's out of school. If we do have a child, it won't slow us up. We'd like to live upstate in New York or Connecticut. We can talk well together. We've never fought to the point of not speaking. However, we can both be easily hurt by each other.

Case I (Miss A)

My family approves of this. He and my brother get along very well. (How important would it be if your family didn't approve?) I don't know what I'd do. I feel my parents know me. I would listen very carefully. My family means a great deal to me. They have a great influence on me. (Your mother or your father?) My mother—she offers her opinions more. I listen to my father too. Bobby [her fiancé] comes from a large family. His mother died when he was eleven. I don't recall her. His father is a retired accountant. I'm sheltered from him because he's an alcoholic. I'm only with him on certain occasions. We have talked. Nothing personal. I'm old enough to be aware, not frightened. Bobby and his father don't get along, though they live together. He [Bobby's father] doesn't take too great an interest in the marriage. (Can you give me more of a picture of Bobby?) He tries to be self-sufficient. He weighs his opinions carefully. He is not as influenced as me. There are fields where I'm just creeping out into the world from underpants. Bobby has his own opinions. He makes up his mind. To me he's intelligent, impatient to get ahead. (How do you feel about the work he's doing?) He seems to like it. I don't understand it. It's not my field. I like it. I'm not against it. I'm not wishing he'd be doing something else. He takes an interest in it. That's all that's important to me. He's willing to tell me about it, but I feel I'll never get to know a lot. (What is it you feel you want in a man?) Someone to be understanding, who can overcome a lot. If I'm upset, I want him to understand, not to get rattled about the things I do. That's an important difference between a man and a woman. This he has to a degree. At times, not. It's normal. He tries to help me. He's never had anyone to talk to. In the last couple of years more and more comes out. He never had a mother. We discuss everything but his father. He doesn't wish to discuss his father. (Well, what else about Bobby?) He's kind, gentle, he's ambitious. I wouldn't want him to be content. I want him to be more inquisitive. He's that way now. I want him to stand on his own two feet. He's more self-confident. He can tell me to stand up and face the world. He's sensitive to other people. (Anything about him you don't like so much, any weaknesses?) Well, his reticence to change his opinion, not that I try to bend him. He feels I'm influenced by mother. I am. We've discussed this. My mother has lived longer. I do revere her suggestions. (For example?) Oh, about

19

how to handle money. My father gives my mother money for the house. He takes care of the rent, taxes, and gives her for the house and children. Bobby feels my father should take care of the money. I'm working and have a salary. He says we should put my money in the bank. We agree to save. He doesn't feel like me, that you live once. He wants my salary to go in the bank. If I mention it in connection with home, if I say Mom and Dad do so and so, he feels I'll run home to mother. It would be hard for me to move to California because my parents are here. He's thought of moving there. He has the feeling I'd be running home. (Would you move to California if he gets a job offer there?) I'm not sure. I could move to a nearby state. I have close family ties. That's not wrong. I don't understand his feeling.

(Have you dated much?) A good deal. (What about sexual experience?) I had offers, a few ticklish experiences. I went to visit a girl friend in Miami. [She related a long circumstantial incident where there was at least a possibility of her getting sexually involved.] (How do you feel about having sexual relations?) My feeling is, "Don't." I have a conscience. If I were promiscuous I'd be hurting myself. I see my classmates. They're very different. One man after another. With them it's O.K., not for me. Bobby and I have talked together about this. What keeps me now from going back on my morals is that I waited so long, and the fear of pregnancy. (Does he press you about this?) There was a time he did. He doesn't want to press me now since I told him how I feel. I feel it would influence me greatly. Then we don't have really time alone. We go to the movies or a show and don't spend time alone. He knew how I felt. It would be a farce. We're alone occasionally, but our time is occupied. Now I've changed. I don't feel it would be so wrong because I'm very much in love with him and sure of his love. A year ago I wasn't as sure of his love. (Do you feel he isn't particularly eager also to have sexual relations now?) I know he's never had intercourse. I don't know. I don't want particularly to discuss it with him. We've waited so long, we can wait five months longer. (Do you fear there would be a risk to your relationship if you were sexually involved with Bobby?) No, no risk. It would be immoral. You're not supposed to. (Do you feel a desire for sexual relations with him?) Yes. (Do you worry if sex will be a problem?) I wonder how things will work out. Whether I'll be capable of satisfying him. (Where did you get your feeling about sex?) All from my mother. My mother explained to me about menstruation. She told me about this too. She brought in God. She told me it's beautiful between a husband and wife. If you did it otherwise, it wouldn't be as nice because it's wrong. I've discussed it with her. She knows I'm not involved with Bobby sexually. She asked me and she wanted to tell me again how she felt. She told me when I got an apartment last July. She said if I hadn't made up my mind it would be easier. Through the years my mother has always been my conscience. (What did she say?) I was never punished since I was a little girl. (What about self-stimulation?) No, they said in class it was normal. I asked my mother and she said, I never did. She said no. (Did you ever do it later?) No. (Did you ever desire to?) No. (Would that be wrong?) In a moral sense, no. I don't know if it's wrong or right. I don't like to see little children clutching themselves. If a child of mine did it, I'd divert it. [END OF SESSION.]

One or two recurrent themes are worth noting here. There is in every session a person who is "a skeleton in the family closet." Of course her preoccupation with this must come from her own brother, but it occurs in discussing her grandmother, her teacher with a schizophrenic daughter, and now Bobby's father. Her dependent, almost symbiotic tie to her mother is most noteworthy. It influences her attitude toward marrying or not marrying her boy friend, toward sexual relations, etc. She is a girl who reveals a good deal through her choice of words: she "reveres" her mother's suggestions; she doesn't like to see little children "clutching themselves," etc.

The degree of her disapproval of sexual relations was unusual. With none of the other girls could one imagine such an attitude persisting through a three-year engagement. This is undoubtedly also related to the sort of boy she would choose —a fact that becomes clearer later.

Fourth Interview

[She was asked at the beginning of the fourth interview what she felt were her biggest problems.] Mainly that I'm oversensitive, apprehensive. I fear I won't measure up. Whom am I trying to impress? (Whom do you think?) Could be people, could be myself. I do feel my mother is almost a conscience to me. My mother's likes and dislikes seem to govern me a

21

great deal. I seem insecure. I don't know why it should be. It goes back to kindergarten. (How do you account for it in kindergarten?) Well, I really had it before kindergarten. My mother tells me as a child I was easily bowel-trained. I'd have my bowel movement the same time each day. I walked at ten months. At about two I rebelled against something. I wouldn't move my bowels except at inopportune times. The pediatrician said I needed to get away from my mother for a week and a half. I went to the hospital. It was the only time I was ever separated from my parents except when my brother was born. Parts I remember of the hospital are pleasant. Must have been O.K. I know one thing. It cured me of the difficulty. (Don't you think you were frightened out of it?) Well, perhaps. [Ten seconds silence.] I try to go home as often as possible. I know my parents want me home. I'm torn between feelings, where should my allegiance be, how will it change when I am married. Yet I want to break with them. My mother feels I should wait another year to get married. She hasn't really said that. (Is there any possibility you'll wait?) Well, there's no reason to. (What do you feel are your mother's weaknesses?) She's a nervous type, not easygoing. Little things bother her. She had a hysterectomy eleven years ago. She's always excitable and reduced to tears easily. (By what?) Harsh words. (From whom?) My father mostly. Not arguing. Just tensions. Things mount up. I'm very much like that. My fiancé has said that my mother has an iron fist over my father, that he does all for her. This seems strange to me. My mother doesn't yell. She's little. She speaks kindly. My father is influenced by her. (Do you feel she's the stronger?) Yes, she is. My mother is my conscience. She dictates how I should feel. My mother talks and I listen. My brother rebels. He started to rebel when he was a little boy. Mother would say, "Sit in the chair," and he wouldn't do it. He got a lot of spankings. He only did things boys do. He's a devilish kid. I can't say if it was my mother's fault or my brother's. He felt badly about all the things he said to my mother. He got more punishment. He was denied things; he'd get spanked. I never recall being punished. A sharp word would be my punishment. Difficulties with my brother started when he was eleven. He had to have a tutor come in. At that age it seemed insurmountable that he couldn't learn to read. We were in the same school. I was told to watch out for him. He was a model child at the school.

Case I (Miss A)

At home he was uproarious, in open rebellion. (Was your brother withdrawn?) No, he was outspoken, loud. He'd tell you what he'd do. (How did he act toward you?) I was a problem. I set too fast a pace for him. He was always trying to live up to me. (How did he behave toward you?) We got along well. We had our fights. I don't see too much wrong with him today. (Do you ever feel ashamed about him?) No, there's nothing to see. At times he's docile. Too much excitement makes him unruly. He doesn't come home except Christmas and for spring and summer vacations. He loves it there. He really does. My mother wouldn't tolerate disobedience but she shows displeasure in a very mild way. [END OF SESSION.]

The picture given by her fiancé and confirmed by her of her mother dominating her father is new, but not surprising. Her brother rebelled against the mother's domination, and, as has been indicated, the subject seems to see his emotional disturbance as a partial consequence. She is torn in deciding how much her mother should be blamed. She herself appears to have been frightened early in life into adopting a dependent, submissive attitude toward her mother. This makes it difficult for her to see her mother with any objectivity, and it seems that her mother is more disturbed than the subject realizes. Indeed the subject's own dependent and submissive attitude may have been the only possible adaptation that would have worked.

Fifth Interview

Since last time I did have a dream: I gave Pat, a colored orderly, a shot of some narcotic. The supervisor came around. I was in haste to cover it up. I put him in bed. I felt, if she asks, I'll say he's sick. I went around changing the books. I gave another man atropine and said it was a narcotic. No one said anything.

I had the dream Sunday. Saturday night we had been discussing this other orderly whom we think may be an addict. Pat, one of the orderlies on the ward, another nurse, and I had been talking about him, but the orderly in the dream actually was Pat. The supervisor hadn't been around all night that night. We had coffee and were on the lookout for her. In the dream I shoved him in bed and closed the door. (Did anything else happen on Saturday?) That night at work all was quiet. (What about before work?) We didn't go out. I was working the night shift. Bobby came over at 8:30. We discussed things for the apartment. He went home around 11 or 11:30. We were mainly talking about pictures, and I told him I picked up one. Also my aunt had a mastectomy and I'm going to help her out. The rest of the day, I was pleased with it. We had discussed my insecurity. It was out in words, and I agreed. [She was referring to the last interview which took place the morning before the dream.] I talked to my roommate about it on Saturday. She has the same sort of problem. (What about the narcotics in the dream?) A few weeks ago there was a case, an exploratory laparotomy. He got adhesions, I felt his illness was psychosomatic. This doctor gives narcotics very freely. One woman getting demerol. I don't usually question, but I just couldn't picture her in that much pain. I refused to give that much demerol. She was calling for it every two hours. I spoke to the doctor again. I was very snappy. I told the doctor that the order should be changed. I felt I was in the right. He refused to change and I gave a sterile hypo one night. However, I told him about it later. I felt guilty for taking it upon myself. However, she responded to the hypo. She said she liked it. It made her relax. (What are your feelings toward Pat?) He's helpful. I don't know him well. He makes coffee. He does what you ask. He mumbles a little. He's one of the nicer orderlies. (Whom might Pat represent in your life?) Could it be Bobby? He never professed a desire for narcotics. All he asked to do on Saturday was to go to Masters. (Well, what about narcotics?) Well, narcotics are to relieve pain. The way I dreamed it, however, it would be more for pleasure. I always felt it would be more of a sickening pleasure. Oh, gee, that doesn't sound too good. [It was clear here the patient had made an association between her last remarks and her feelings about sex. She immediately went on.] You know, I had a phallic dream in which Bobby was scaring me with a penknife. He was running around with it. I told him I couldn't see him. That people were talking. I told my roommate about the dream. She said I shouldn't tell it to you. (Who do you think the supervisor was in the first dream?) My mother. Last time I said Mother was stronger than my father. (Is this true of you in relation to Bobby?) I went with guys heretofore where

Case I (Miss A)

I had the upper hand. With Bobby I don't feel as strong. He's more dominant. I can't get away with saying any old thing. He wants to know why, how can you say that. I fought hard to keep a footing. I don't feel a woman should be docile and led around.

[Her association to Pat had been that of an orderly who always did what you told him. This appeared a truer picture of how she saw her relationship with Bobby than her conscious attempt to state otherwise. The reaction to sex as frightening and to Bobby as having a penknife as represented in the dream needs little discussion. Interesting, too, is her connection of sexual pleasure with the pleasure of a narcotic, pleasurable but illicit, addicting, sickening. On the other hand, in the dream she is defying her mother and having something to do with sex, although it is evidently necessary for her to maintain control and be in the phallic role in order to participate. The story of her defiance of the doctor's order by giving a sterile hypo points in the same direction.]

(How attractive do you feel you are?) Oh, please, I didn't feel I was the ugliest. When I was eleven, I had acne, eighteen, nineteen and twenty I had a cystic type of acne. It started to pit my skin. It's calmed down now. It's not completely gone. I hope it's on the way out. I felt if I hadn't had that, I'd be more outgoing. Licking it by sheer force. I always had a boy friend. They went and came. I think it caused me not to be asked by some. (I have the feeling that you weren't satisfied with your attractiveness even before the acne.) Oh, that's true. That was partially to do with my fear to get up on stage. However, I did on occasion.

[She went on to speak of her theatrical experiences in plays and of her playing the piano. The last session closed with the interviewer asking about her plans. She thought after she had married she'd stay for another year at the hospital, then get a house. She didn't want any children until they were out of the city. In response to a question she indicated that as far as having a child, her preference was for a boy.] [END OF SESSION.]

It is difficult to assess whether this subject's well-controlled defenses would in the normal course of living ever break sufficiently to cause either neurotic or paranoid complaints. Her control of her underlying pathology appeared to be very good, and one is inclined to think that she is managing, and will continue to do so, the kind of relationship that she can handle. Yet even if she can avoid difficulty when she marries and begins a sexual relationship, there is the danger that her adaptation may be threatened by her mother's death.

Her relative freedom from current problems made her even more instructive from the standpoint of psychoanalytic interviewing. For despite the absence of serious pathology she revealed in five hours, through the use of free association, dreams, and occasional interpretations, as much as one would hope to get from an actual patient in the same length of time.

CASE II

(*Miss B*)

In the next two cases only the initial sessions are reported in detail and the subsequent sessions are summarized. In both, the basic psychodynamics were already strongly suggested in the first session, and the subsequent sessions clarified and confirmed the initial pictures.

Miss B was a twenty-three-year-old good-looking, well-built girl. While she was feminine in appearance, her carriage had a gawky, adolescent quality, and she made broad hand gestures in talking. After a minute or two of introductory remarks in which she told where she had lived and who was in her family she proceeded as follows:

I'm sure you want personality. It's best that I tell it with anecdotes. I'm an adventure lover, and I like people—at times I get disgusted with them. Our parents have always trusted us. We never hesitated telling them what we did. Wouldn't take advantage of them, it would ruin it for us for the next time. When I was sixteen I was allowed to take my driving license. My sister is a year and a half younger, and we spent that

27

summer by ourselves in our first summer place. We met very different people. We were near a summer camp for problem children. This camp, they did all kinds of things. It was a kind of experiment in human relations, and I became interested. When I was in training I'd go down town and pick up people and talk to them. I got into trouble at C [her psychiatric training affiliation]. The world is psychologically oriented. We were there to be observed, whether we knew it or not. I used to talk to the young toughs in the neighborhood. I trusted them. That's really all you have to do. I was in command. I felt they were more willing to talk to me than to a forty-year-old man or woman. They wouldn't say the same things. I wouldn't forget what they said. In conference I mentioned my talking to these young toughs and the nurse in charge said that Dr. A [the psychiatrist there] was interested. It was a trick. It was clear that I was on the couch. Excuse me for saying it, but he was a highly nervous man. He asked me if I could refrain from seeing this crowd. They had visions of me raped in a ditch. (Just what were you doing?) Well, at C they get ideas. One time they had the idea that I was in love with the patient. I've been told that I'm quite, quote, "seductive," unquote. By treating them normally, I got a normal response. I pat a woman on the back to tell her to stand up straight, I was told I was arousing her homosexuality. I was told I was stealing this man's affection. I felt like saying: "From whom?"

I felt the nursing teacher was mature enough so that I could say what I said. I never thought what she'd make of it. I came back from this counseling session [with the psychiatrist], and he declared me sane. We chatted and had a good time. He gave me books. He said: "Come back." I was embarrassed to, since I forgot the name of the books. I overwhelmed him.

[She appeared to be using her past experience with a psychiatrist to reveal rather rapidly both her expectations of the present interviewer as well as the means she would use to deal with him. There was a somewhat paranoid quality to her remarks about being "observed" and it being a "trick," as well as a grandiose quality to her feeling of "being in command" with delinquents and her feeling that she "overwhelmed" the hospital psychiatrist.]

I'm impulsive. I do things on impulse. Most people don't dare to. I don't fear to be rejected because I make a fool of myself. I constantly do. I don't care what people think. (Impulsive?) My first trip to Boston with my sister we went into tough hangouts. I was told that to go into a den of lions is not wise. I never feared a human being and never will. I feel if someone says they will kill me, just give me five minutes and I'll talk them out of it.

I like to be alone most of the time. I don't like women too well. They are shallow. Four or five women in the room and they immediately talk about things that bore me. Most of my good friends are men. Had them for years. For many years I was one of the boys. I had to check in with them when I went downtown that I was back all right. It was silly. I was just like a kid sister. They were upset when I gave blood.

I was a tomboy. Helped my mother with my sister. My mother was worried that anything might happen to my sister. [This was said slightly bitterly if ironically.] My sister and I are close. I didn't like dolls long. My sister's main concern was dolls, besides the animals we had. She is more feminine. But we're alike. I guess it's a garbled mess. I free-associate very well. I don't think I'll ever have an ulcer because of not letting things out, then you run into trouble. Best cure-all is sleep. If I'm cold or emotionally upset I go to sleep.

I've a terrible temper. I must keep it under control at all times or it frightens me. (What do you mean?) Oh, I reach a point of anger that if I had something I would have killed without remorse. (Well, when does that happen?) Oh, this boy was telling me problems about another girl, attacking women in general. I retaliated with anger. I'd like a chance for a good brawl. I get angry about prejudice or injustice. Have to wait to do anything. You must have power or money to do anything. My father used to work on the waterfront, and I know a lot about the shady side of life. I chain-smoke, incidentally.

[She then told what appeared to be a partially true and partly paranoid story involving the hospital administration. It involved her being both defender of the oppressed, a martyr herself, and eventually a victorious heroine, and in this respect was similar to the incident that took place at her psychiatric affiliation. She concluded the session by stating, "I hope I don't shock you too much with what I say."] [END OF SESSION.]

Certainly she was hoping both to shock and to overwhelm the interviewer with her interest in violence, her fearlessness, and her forthrightness. Words like "kill," "murder," and

29

"brawl" run through the session. She must control her temper, since when she gets angry enough she feels she could kill. At times she was dramatic and engaging, at times seemingly cocky and affectedly casual—all of these qualities only partly covered the paranoid tone of both her mistrust and her grandiosity.

She made it clear that her identification was with men, that she had contempt for women, and that she had been a tomboy and wanted masculine freedom in all her behavior. She contrasted this with her sister's more feminine concerns, and appeared to imply greater interest on the part of her mother for her sister.

In the second session she reported a recurrent dream that she had had since high school, which troubled her: "There is a long, flat, desolate road, trees without leaves and ditches, and there are marching soldiers. I'm in a ditch. As they go by they do something characteristic of them. They smile. I know all of them. Then they are all dying, and I cannot do anything. One time I had that dream for a week running. The helpless feeling bothered me most. After I was in training, in the second part of that dream I'd be a nurse and I still couldn't do anything."

She went on to say: "I want to tell you something about ESP that will interest you," and proceeded to relate several experiences that she considered potentially telepathic. She then continued:

"The most important thing in life is love. It should be there. Diseased minds are without it. I don't know how to hate. I can become angry, but I can't keep it. I'm done with it. I don't seek revenge. Love conquers all. Even the most disagreeable. If a person with a gun comes around you can get them to say good morning. The young delinquents—I trusted them. They were so overwhelmed they didn't know what to do. They never did anything. I wanted to find out what they did. They were cynical. They didn't care. No one made them feel it was important to care." (Do you ever think you might go in the delinquent direction?) "Yes, to become more like a stone. But could I kill in a war? If I saw my family butchered. I'd turn to stone and start killing. Lose faith in people. Be like a priest without religion. I understand it in part. I got angry with things. My high school was a typical suburban high school. All kinds were there. Children from broken homes. They were shunned. The faculty did nothing. Italians and Jews were shunned. I was reprimanded for contact with them."

While she did not appear to deal with her war dream directly, her associations following it are revealing. She gave many indications that her need to be the defender of the weak was part of an attempt to control her own aggressive, defiant, destructive impulses. She further continued in the session the same somewhat grandiose, somewhat paranoid trend of her first session.

In the third and fourth sessions she told the story of her family and her childhood. She portrayed her father as a somewhat fussy man who blew off steam when angry, and was a bit of a clown. However, if there was some lack of respect in her image of him, there was a good deal of affection too. She appeared to respect her mother more, but the affectionate tone was missing when she discussed her mother. She elaborated on her mother's closeness to her younger sister and the protective role she herself played toward this sister. She spoke further of her sister as more feminine, more attractive, and as using more feminine wiles in dealing with their father. She said her father wanted a son, and in her description of their common interests she appeared to have adopted a boy's attitudes with regard to him. Her father, however, worked away from home during the period when she was two to five and again during the years when she was eight to twelve. The first time he was working as a seaman; in the second period he did construction work in New York, while they lived in another state. She tried to deny the importance of this separation, but it seemed to reflect some difficulty between the parents, as well as undoubtedly being critical for her growth and development.

One dream that she had during the course of the interviews and reported in the last session is worth noting, since it illustrates both her problem with violence and her fears of the feminine role:

"I was in a barn and was trapped. There were gray and black boars with long tusks. I was along the wall trying to get to the opening to get out. I had a long stick with me as a club. I made it to the opening. I had to use the club. I was frightened I would fall off the edge I was on. The barn was brown with green grass under the opening. The boars were black and gray and bluish."

Even without direct associative evidence, it is reasonable to assume that the boars represent men who are seen as violent and dangerous. The stick suggests that she attempts to master her fears by assuming a phallic role. Even without the dream, there was ample evidence of her fears of the feminine role. Her masculine identification, including her emphasis on being unusual and adventurous, is best understood as a defense against these fears.

It is a little harder to decide the source of her violence and underlying terror of the female role. Her father's absence from the home and his general ineffectiveness were certainly factors. The interviewer had the impression of coolness, distance, and perhaps even rejection on the part of her mother. The progression of information about her mistrustfulness, violence, and grandiosity was most striking. These characteristic features of a paranoid personality were already suggested in the first session by the anecdotes she told as well as by her attitudes toward the interviewer. They received corroboration in the historical data of the second and third session and eventual confirmation from her dreams.

CASE III

(Miss C)

Miss C was tall, neatly dresssed, with nice features, and would have been attractive if she had not been so tremendously overweight. After being told that the investigator wanted a picture of her in her own words, she began as follows:

I am twenty-seven years old, a registered nurse, a graduate of R Nursing School. I went there straight after high school. I've been on my own since high school, and I've had my own apartment. I'm in good health except for being overweight. I've been overweight since I was ten. I was told I was hypo-thyroid and put on thyroid from the age of ten to sixteen. At sixteen I had an overreaction to thyroid and had a heart block. Since then I've been on and off diets. I had to lose twenty-five pounds to get into nursing school and I went from 225 to 195. (How tall are you?) Five feet ten inches. I never thought my weight was a problem till I got here. They've put on a drive to get me to lose weight every six months or so. I have no real incentive. I went to Dr. N [the psychiatric consultant at the hospital]. I gave the right answers.

I saw him once a week for almost a year, and I still didn't lose any weight. I smoke a lot, three packs a day.

As far as nursing, I didn't aspire to be a nurse. I wished to be a teacher. I have a sister one year younger than myself. My father said he could only put one of us through college. I decided to take a job instead with a company. The work was easy, and I was told that I shouldn't work so hard and I should work at a slower pace. A doctor at home advised me to try nursing. I applied to three hospitals. I was turned down at T because of my weight. I liked the studies, but I was unhappy the first six months. I didn't like orders. I had been free. The instructors didn't seem human. Now I understand the system. But then my father had to bring me here on weekends to get me to go back.

When I was a senior a student told me that I was shy. I haven't been since. [She laughed at this. The remark, however, suggested a mechanical quality to her behavior.] I'm outgoing. I don't let things bother me. I don't put off things except for a day. I won't charge things in a store. In the hospital I'm a head nurse, and I handle the responsibility well. It doesn't bother me. Outside of the hospital I'm only bothered if I hear someone doesn't like me. I don't know why. I've had four or five medical friends. My other friends are casual friends from home. My sister, I live with her now, followed me into nursing school. She didn't go on to college. At home we used to fight continuously. Now we get along very well.

I like head nursing. My plan is to remain a head nurse, despite efforts to get me to be a supervisor. I've gotten marvelous reports for five years. It's nice to know you're so wonderful. I don't wish to be a teacher or supervisor. I don't want to go to school. This hospital is set up for bedside nursing, and that's what I want. I disagree with the change of three- to five-year program by the National Nurses League. Degree nurses, you have to teach them how to care for a patient. They follow the rules, and the rules don't apply to a real situation. They're a pain in the neck. Most of the head nurses here are not degree nurses. I'd like to be a head nurse in the future like I am now. The pay is good, double what it was when I started. Money doesn't mean that much to me. I never had much in the bank. I enjoy theaters, not spending on clothes. I'm a great gift buyer. I'm satisfied with what I

make. As far as marriage and a family, I want it, but it's not
the end of everything. It would be nice to have one great
love and be married and that's it. I'm not very religious, but
I don't believe in divorces. Earlier I used to go out with men
once, twice a week. I've been told that I'd go out more if I
lost weight.

[She smiled.] I'm stymied. I like living in the city. I
wouldn't live elsewhere. I was brought up in the country, but
I don't like it any more. My pet peeve is being called Mother.
I'm not that personality type. Most of my friends call me that
because of my size. I'm supposed to be a stabilizing influence
in a group. I don't give advice or criticize. As head nurse
that's the hardest thing to learn. If I was a patient, perhaps
I'd be quick to criticize, perhaps too much so. When I began,
I was so critical, the group reported me as being too demand-
ing. I was called down. Then I was too friendly and was
walked over. Then I was severe again and I was reported.
[Again a kind of mechanical doing and undoing was suggested.] Now I've found a happy medium. I get along with
people. I don't like any of the people I work with. One aide
is dependent and an alcoholic. I don't dislike her, but I'm
more and more intolerant. She worked for years, and they
wish to keep her. She's out often and very dependent when
she is in. One orderly is not honest. You leave the floor and
he relaxes. I feel you work eight hours and those eight hours
you should work. I give them fifteen minutes off in the after-
noon, but I like to get the work done. The assistant head
nurse is peculiar. She was cheerful as a student but anything
but that now. The doctors don't like her. She's bossy, intolerant, and tactless. She calls me by my first name in front of the
patients. I don't call her that. I don't believe in it. Another
graduate on the ward thinks she knows it all. The nursing unit
assistant is an older woman in her forties. The job is too much
for her. She doesn't understand what I want. None of them
realize that I don't like them. I make an effort to keep the
peace.

My mother and father are two lovely people. [She laughed.]
They don't understand what's going on in the world, but
they're nice—compatible. We had no problems. They like
each other's company. They stay home at night. My father
comes here to visit, and he feels why don't I work in an office
[doctor's office] like my sister. My parents don't discuss re-

35

ligion or go to church. They don't discuss the world situation.
My father has an important job. Other than that, he just likes
to take his boat out on weekends. My mother works in a small
office. She started working after we graduated from high
school to have money for clothes. I seldom go home. I'm
bored. I go home and take a ride. In the city I'm only in my
apartment five hours and that just to sleep, yet when I'm
home [at her parents'] I don't smoke. I think when I'm nervous
I smoke more. My father doesn't like overweight people. He
thinks they're lazy and sloppy. He and my mother are average height and weight. The more he prodded me, the more I
gained. I went to nursing school; he resigned himself to my
being fat. My sister has been between 148 and 200 pounds.
The last two years she's been thin. She was skinny as a child.
In nursing school her eating habits went berserk.

I don't like family gatherings. I don't like my relatives.
I've avoided them for seven years. [She puts her hands in
her pockets now while she talks.] I had too much of them as
a kid. I always hear criticism, why don't I come home more
often. My aunt lost her job. She's in her fifties. She wants me
to help her find a job. I don't like family gatherings. I don't
like small talk. I don't like gossip. I like to discuss boats or
current events or sports. Housework leaves me cold. I don't
do it. We both hate housework. I hate to go to the beauty
parlor. I like to read four or five books at once. I read for the
story. I don't like eighteenth- or seventeenth-century set-
tings. I don't like the classics. I like modern work. I only go
to the movies to see a funny picture. Nothing with a deep
meaning, or thought-provoking. Occasionally I like a spec-
tacular like *Ben-Hur*. Also movies about operas are all right,
the story has to go with them, otherwise I like just to be en-
tertained. TV, I only like the news broadcasts and sports. I
enjoy records. If I did it over, I'd do things the same way.
(What do you mean?) Well, maybe not about the weight. If
I knew about the weight when I was younger, I'd lose it then.
But I'd go through nursing school again. I like that best, except maybe flying a jet. (You appear to accept your weight
now in a rather resigned way.) I don't have the time to diet.
I went on Metrecal, lost forty pounds, had a GI upset. With
working it's very difficult to stick to a diet. (No time?) At
night my best girl friend and I do everything together. We've
been doing it for years. She likes all the activities I do. She

whether this was true when they were both children, she responded: "No, then we were treated equally. As a matter of fact, I was the one who had to help. Mother said I was a year older. My sister never helped. She was in more activities. She'd be home later. She'd miss supper and wasn't reprimanded. They were worried about her not eating or sleeping. My sister and mother talked more together. They'd gossip. My sister goes home every weekend."

She went on further to describe the greater closeness that existed between her mother and sister. The subject's own tomboy interests as a child were not those of her father either. She described her mother as more lively than her father, but evidently felt neither parent expressed much affection or interest in her. Her parents kept to themselves and had few friends. Her father came across as rigid, wrapped up in work, and capable of little pleasure or warmth. She reiterated her boredom with her parents while saying that she had no real complaint with them. At the same time she was bitter toward the world and had rejected the feminine role. As has been noted, her obesity was part of this rejection and contributed to her abandoning hope of ever achieving satisfaction as a woman. While she had had one sexual affair with a married doctor, she now seldom dated. She stated again that she wasn't that concerned as to whether or not she married and appeared to have resigned herself to not doing so. She worked night shifts and extra duty and kept busy with work as a way of avoiding having to face her problems. She saw marriage as involving "a lot of giving in, and this means giving a lot" and she evidently saw "giving" and "giving in" as the same thing. She was sure she could bring up children, but not sure how much love she could give them. Her gross affective incapacity and the extent of her retreat from the role of a woman indicate the severity of her emotional pathology.

Miss C managed to convey a complete psychodynamic picture in one hour. She presented her obesity as her "only" problem, and indeed, it had become the symbolic focus for numerous other conflicts as well as her basic defense in life. She revealed most of the psychoanalytic meanings of her obesity, and in so doing revealed herself.

CASE IV

(Miss D)

In the next case, the first two sessions are summarized, with later sessions reported in greater detail. This case is especially revealing in demonstrating the value of judicious challenging by the interviewer of contradictions in the diverse implications of what the subject is reporting. In this particular example, the subject's defenses were readily revealed.

Miss D was a twenty-five-year-old pale, blond girl who, while not particularly attractive, managed to make the most of her physical appearance and to generate an air of attractiveness. She had the grooming and manner that one associates with a higher economic level than that of most of the other nurses. She talked in an expressionless way, and her face had almost a masklike quality. She seemed shy but peculiarly self-confident.

In the first interview, the subject discussed her family and family background. She indicated she had always been shy as a child, although she remembered having a small circle of close friends. She described her father as generally quiet, although she said that when guidance was needed, he gave it. When he talked, others listened. It was suspected at the time that, while consciously referring to her father, she was unconsciously alluding to the interviewer's silence and interpreting it as similar to that of her father. This expression of transference, that is, the endowment of the relatively neutral interview relationship with characteristics and emotions of a significant childhood relationship, was confirmed in later interviews.

Her mother was described as more vivacious and emotionally expressive than her father. The subject felt she herself was more like her father, particularly in the area of controlling her temper. However, she stated that she and her mother and her younger sister were all different from her father in that they were stubborn and had more will power. She described the family's strong Roman Catholic religious convictions, although an underlying conflict with them might be suggested by the fact that she had selected a nonsecular nurse's training center because of "wanting exposure to other groups" and the belief that "if religion is pushed too much it tends to sour people."

The subject began the second interview by discussing her dating experiences. When asked explicitly about sexual experiences she avoided answering until questioned again. (This is very hard to talk about?) "Yes, very. It was the way it was taught. It is very hard for me to talk about anything that is important. I don't know what it is. I don't think it is specifically just the sexual thing, although it may be, but anything that means a great deal to me is hard for me to talk about to someone else." (Would you rather we didn't talk about this aspect of your life?) "I don't know. I'm not sure. In many ways I think it's good that you're asking me about this. Maybe I'll learn something as far as sex is concerned." She then indicated that although she and her boy friend engaged in petting, she did not have intercourse because of her religious convictions. She added that the fear of pregnancy also served as a restriction. She stated that, nonetheless, she was very passionate and was afraid she might lose control.

She then proceeded to describe her current boy friend, a builder. "I'm very fond of him. I have known him for years. I think I'm in love with him. He wants to marry me, but he hasn't established himself. I don't feel he makes enough money to support a wife and children." (How much does he make?) "Around $8000–$9000." (Isn't that enough to marry on?) She smiled. "That's because of something I haven't told you. I'm terribly spoiled. My mother says I have it too good at home, that I'll never leave it."

Miss D began her third hour by asking where she had left off in the previous session. She then talked about how she was spoiled as a child and how her parents tried to anticipate her every want. She continued by telling about her studies and experiences in high school. She was unclear as to how she happened to go into nursing. She indicated that if she had to do it over again, she would choose other work. She was disenchanted with nursing and considered it dull. (If it is such a bore, why continue?) "When I seriously wanted to go, there was no one to take my place. I'm just in a rut; I feel I'm in a rut with my friends. My roommate and I both talk about leaving. I'd like to go somewhere warm—California or Hawaii. Actually, I don't know what I want. I've been offered a job traveling. I thought I might take it. I would like to see a little before I settle down." (When you say settle down, do you mean with Joe?) "I presume so. He seems to fill most of my needs." (That doesn't sound terribly romantic.) "I've known him so long. I wonder if it's a habit. If I found out he was going to marry someone else, I suppose that would disturb me. Yes, it would very much. I think I would be happy with him." (Well, what is it you want from life?) "I want to be married, I want to have children, I want to have a home, etcetera." (Well, why don't you?) "I have trouble growing up and settling down. I would have to give up plays, concerts, fine restaurants, etc. We couldn't afford it. I want to spoil my children the way I was. I want four children. I'd like a house in the country. When I first moved to the city I hated it. It took me three years to get used to liking it. I couldn't say I adjusted rapidly. I like a comfortable life. I'd like enough money to educate the children. I would make my children go on to school. I wouldn't discourage my daughters if they wanted to go into nursing, but I certainly wouldn't encourage them. Maybe I'm just tired of working. Certainly the last couple of years I've been tired. Nursing does have a certain prestige in the layman's eyes. Nurses now seem not to care enough, not interested in doing good work. Maybe I'm a perfectionist. The young ones are sloppy, they leave things undone. They're less dedicated. They don't plan on staying this long. They plan on getting married. It's just an interlude, but then again, isn't it true for me too?" (If you are bored and you have someone that you are in love with and you say that your ultimate goal is marriage, why don't you get married?) "I don't know, I don't seem to make a convincing case in what I say, do I? He doesn't have the education I want in a husband. I want a husband I can look up to. I feel we're more or less on the same level. Yet I've gone out with boys with graduate degrees and they lack a quality that he has. He's understanding, he'd make a good father. He'd be kind with children, he's serious-minded. Maybe I really need an older man. I seem to enjoy dating older men. I can talk better with them. He's bright, but he doesn't apply himself. He's two years older. He's not ambitious, there's no push, there's no drive."

It had been apparent in this session that the subject was much less composed than appeared at first. A growing dissatisfaction, bordering on a moderate depression, was evident. It was interesting to note that her attitude about her boy friend changed when challenged by the obvious fact that she claimed to love him yet refused to marry him at a time when she was looking for a change in her life. As the hour went on, her dissatisfaction with the boy became much more overt in expression. It appeared that the escape she wanted was from him and whatever he represented to her, which at this time was not clear. Every time she was challenged and pressed about her contradictory statements, the nature of her associations changed. There was an increased show of emotion and spontaneity. While she always talked fluently, her associations became less planned and exposed more. In this session, the interviewer's challenges apparently reached her and elicited a strong response.

The subject was forced to miss a session because of schedule change and then came in for her fourth session. She talked about the missed session and said she was sorry because she had lots to tell. Now she had nothing to report. With encouragement, she recalled a dream she had had two weeks before. "I was at a flower show. I met an attending doctor from the hospital." Her one association was to the flower show she had attended with Joe on her most recent date with him and their meeting a doctor from the hospital ward. She was questioned about the specific doctor. "He's an older man. He's Catholic. He knows my pastor. He keeps telling me to get out of the hospital. It's going to make an old biddy out of me. I wonder if he is right. I have changed. I used to be happy-go-lucky, but I'm not any more. It's depressing on the ward where I am. Six out of ten cases are cancer cases. You get to know them and the family. I go home at night almost knocked out. It's hard not to identify. It's hard not to be hurt by what's happening to them. I'd like a livelier floor." (Why not change?) "There's no one to take my place. I may leave in April. I think I will leave. I may take the summer off—I may go home and just loll and spoil myself—I may travel." She explained that she lived in a resort area where it was very enjoyable in the summer. She found friends, there was a chance to date a great deal, swim, etc. "Then maybe after the summer, I'll get a more interesting job." (Are you enjoying life?) "No, I'm too tired. I think I'm basically a lazy and spoiled person." (What do you want to give you pleasure?) "Not much more than settling down and raising a family." (Well, then?) "I was thinking when you asked the question about Joe and why I didn't marry him. It is strange."

At this point the interviewer had a feeling about the meaning of the dream. The paucity of emotion and action in the dream, however, leaves it open to question. The dream was associated with her last date with Joe. The only other association she combined with it was that of a mentor telling her that she ought to make a break or change in her life. While she related this to the nursing situation, it seemed even more probable that she was talking about her relationship with Joe.

"When I was thinking about Joe and why I didn't marry him, I remembered a dream that I had a year ago. You know, I think that I'm afraid to get married. I come from a Catholic family, and even though there were two divorces in my family, I don't think that I would ever be able to get a divorce, on religious convictions. Therefore I feel I have to be sure.

"In the dream I was walking down the aisle with my father, getting married. I said, please, don't make me, Daddy. I turned around and ran away, and he let me go."

There is strong implicit evidence that the recall of this

dream at this time has a specific transference meaning. She had said earlier that her father spoke little, but when he talked people listened. She later indicated that she found it easier to talk to older men; she alluded to a doctor who was urging her to "get out of her rut"; and in the dream she asked her father's permission *not* to marry. All of this points to an equation of her father and the interviewer, in which she is unconsciously pleading with the interviewer to tell her she need not marry Joe. The implicit becomes explicit in her associations to this dream.

"The dream was about a year ago. It was my father because he's always understood my point of view so well. There's pressure from everybody else in the family for me to get married. Aunts are always at me—why am I not married. At one time I could have seen myself marrying Joe. Then, when I met more people, my interest broadened. I began to find a new kind of person, a new kind of life. I began to have doubts." (Were there any special people?) "There was a boy this summer that I felt closer to than I have ever felt to any boy I dated, but there was a religious difference. It made it impossible. His name is Don. He was active, he was bright, he was ambitious. There was lots of drive. I met him in June. The first time I met him I didn't think I liked him. He seemed show-offy, brash. He was a TV director. He seemed Bohemian." She became silent. Her face grew rigid with a peculiar expression on it. (You don't want to talk about this?) She was silent for a few minutes and then said: "Uh, uh." It became obvious that she was controlling tears. (Still painful?) "Yes." At this point tears came to her eyes, but nonetheless she persisted. "I felt I loved him. I last saw him in November. At that point things seemed too serious and too difficult. Marriage was impossible. The religious issue was a strong one. He was Jewish. Catholic and Jewish religions are similar in a way. Both are strict or make demands on the individual. He could not agree to a Catholic marriage because of its requirement with children. As a Catholic, I would not be considered married unless it were in the Church. It wouldn't be necessary for him to change his religion, but the Church requires that he consent that the children be raised Catholic. Most of my friends are Jewish or Protestants. I feel I am very broad-minded with everyone, but I feel that I can't be with myself and my children." She was

obviously deeply and emotionally involved with this man
in a way that she had not been with any other man. When
there was no resolution possible, it was she who took the
initiative and said that she didn't want to see him. Although
the relationship had lasted only a few months, it had been
very intense. "After the original breakoff, I knew that he
was going to call. I knew that if I talked to him even once, I
would weaken. The attraction was so strong. I wanted him
so badly. So I made it my business not to be home on the
nights when I knew that he would call. I don't like talking
about this because I'm going to cry. I don't like people to
see my emotions." At this point she began to cry seriously
and cried for a few minutes. "How did you ever get me to
talk about Don? I've told no one about this. I've tried not
even to think about it." (Do you think that it may be this
rather than work that's depressing you?) "It might be. Ever
since then I've wanted to get a change. I've wanted to leave
the job. I know that it was the right decision because both of
us are very stubborn about the things we believe in deeply.
It was amazing that we got along so well. I'm not at all sorry
about having the relationship. It showed me the kind of feelings I'm capable of having and the kind I want with a man.
I'm very fond of Joe, but I don't feel that way at all toward
him. I don't feel he's a strong personality. I feel if I married
him I would end up pushing him through life. I don't mind
helping, but I don't want to push. It's strange, but I think
nurses have a way of attracting weaker men. I talk to the
other nurses and they seem to say the same thing. It seems
like eight out of ten men want a mother rather than a wife.
I really feel as I talk about it now that I've outgrown Joe.
He was in Europe—in service—and didn't see anything, didn't
learn anything, didn't grow. He might just as well have stayed
at home. Even the sexual experience seemed more natural and
easier with Don."

At this point the session had run well over its hour, and
she was told that the time was up. "I had another dream. Do
you want to hear it?" (Yes, but that will have to wait until
next time. Be sure to remember it.) "I'll never understand
how you wheedled these things out of me. It's peculiar. I
might have thought I was hypnotized or something. I've told
you things I haven't told my roommate, my mother, or some
things that I didn't even want to tell myself."

Despite the fact that the subject became upset in the session, the interviewer had the distinct feeling that she was relieved. There was the implication that she had been struggling against considerable family pressure to marry, and the further implication, in the dream, that a strong attachment to her father might make all available boys seem inadequate. It was felt, however, that the implications of this kind of Oedipal involvement could not and should not be introduced to her conscious knowledge at such a late stage of the interview process.

Since the nurses in this study were not patients, there was no purpose in giving them such insights. Without a continuing therapeutic relationship the insights could not be put to practical use, nor could they really be fully understood. They would only frighten and disturb. There is no sense in shattering an individual's illusions or defenses unless one hopes to replace them with superior adaptations.[1]

The dream for which there had been no time in the fourth session, occupied much of the fifth session. It confirmed a good deal of the speculation of the earlier hour and reveals how one dream can expose almost all of the psychodynamics of an individual subject:

"I was at a party at an attending doctor's house, located in the country in the area where I was raised. I was wandering through the house; I was lost from the general group. I met the doctor's daughter and she showed me the way back to the party, but the party was over already. Then I was caught in a storm. There was lightning and flashes of rain. We were on a terrace which was sheltered, and I made my way back to the doctor and his wife under the sheltered eave.

"Then I was in a theater with my aunt. We got separated and I couldn't find her and I couldn't make my way back. It began to rain again. I was out in the street. Then I came to a long table all set with food. Now it was sunny again. My relatives and friends were sitting around the table. I sat down at the table with my parents and my aunts. Everyone was eating. Then a fellow came over. He was of average height,

---

[1] It might be noted that to the best of our knowledge none of the girls was left depressed, unsettled, or psychologically injured by the interviews. One girl was given courage to seek psychotherapy. This had been something she desired and needed, but previously had considered frightening.

husky, a blue-eyed blond, awkward, inept in manner. He was wearing an apron. I didn't know who he was. He started clearing off the table or something. Everyone was laughing at him. I was embarrassed. Somehow they all wanted to fix me up with him. I was horrified. I ran away. Then I was back in the theater, wandering, trying to find my way back to my seat. I couldn't find my aunt and I couldn't find the box and I went through a maze with all sorts of doors. Then I saw a blonde who looked like the movie actress Doris Day, and she helped me find my way back to my seat."

The dream occurred two days after the missed session. The subject stated that she had been disappointed and angry with herself for missing the session because there was lots she wanted to talk about. The boy in the dream reminded her of one to whom her aunt had introduced her, except in reality he was very proper and neat to the point of being stuffy. She said that she tended to be attracted to lean, darker-haired men, though it was not important. She was asked about the sense of isolation in the dream, the desperateness of being cut off. She said that she liked being alone, that she was not lonely when she was alone. As it was the last session, too much could not be done with the dream, although it seemed obvious to the interviewer that the dream expressed the fear of separation from parental authority, separation from the family, a desire for the shelter and protection of the dependency situation represented by her father and mother. At the same time, her relationship with the boy was tantamount to maintaining her relationship with the parents. To secure food, security, and shelter, she must settle for what she considered an inadequate and degrading relationship. An attempt to interpret at least her need for security and her fear of detachment brought only interested agreement, but no emotional response. The mask of guardedness had returned.

It is significant from the point of view of the study as a whole that this girl, although well-guarded and naturally reticent, in five sessions managed to discuss a love affair she had hidden from friends and family, and faced emotions she had hidden from herself. Most important to the success of the psychoanalytic interviews in this case was the interviewer's willingness to cut through rationalizations and denials by direct confrontation.

It is this peculiar combination of seemingly passive nondirection (silence, which forces the patient to select the subject matter) and active, direct confrontation of the patient with his distortions and defenses that makes the psychoanalytic interview so potent an instrument in exposing unconscious desires and attitudes. It is difficult to imagine any sociological research interested in the motivations for behavior that would not benefit by such psychoanalytic investigation.

CASE V

(Mrs. E)

A common finding in interviewing is the tendency of subjects to present "approved" or "correct" images of their life. Information volunteered early, or elicited by questioning, tends to be stereotyped. The material selected from Mrs. E's interviews focuses on her marriage. In this area she dramatically revealed how free associations can modify early stereotyped presentations.

Mrs. E can best be described by the old-fashioned word, plain. She was thin, mildly awkward, and had a gentle manner. Beneath her quiet self-confidence one could sense the possibility of aggressiveness. Her speech was that of an educated, if not erudite, person.

In the first hour her comments about her husband were limited to the following: "My husband is a college student. I have just been married a year. The only problem I can think of is that I wasn't much of a cook at the beginning, but that doesn't seem to exist any more. My husband quit school, but he went back after marriage. We grew up in the same town

53

together. He's three years older than I am. His mother was my Sunday school teacher."

She did reveal in the first hour a great deal about her parents and the nature of their relationship. "My parents are living. We're a very close family. My parents are very understanding. They aren't terribly strict. I was allowed to have the car at sixteen. My mother was always the one who disciplined me. My father disciplined my brother. People said I was spoiled, but I think the more correct word would be indulged. We were given many material things. We weren't spoiled in that we knew respect for individuals, elders, and parents."

Her father was quite successful. He had a profitable working farm and later was in the produce business. She was raised on a farm until the age of twelve. Her father, now forty-six years old, was a robust man, active in community affairs, the church, and in local athletics. "He is the straw boss in the family."

"He has one obvious fault. He's easygoing and lets people take advantage of his good nature. He would let all deadbeats off the hook and was a soft touch for every sob story. My mother would handle the finances. My father never really criticized me. He would tell my mother and she would tell me. I think I've inherited that from him. It's hard for me to give orders. I would have difficulty being a charge nurse. I feel I'm too easygoing."

She gave the picture of her father as a lovable but quite passive man, whose success was due to his charm and gregariousness, combined with her mother's strength. Her mother is "the backbone of the family financially. She tends to take the initiative. She definitely ran things when I was younger, but in a very quiet way. She never dominated, although she had to take certain things in her hands at certain times."

In the second session Mrs. E returned to discussing her husband at a significant time. Talking about her brother, six and a half years younger, and her maternal attitudes toward him, she said: "Maybe I should go on to my husband while I'm on character sketches. My husband and I are sort of opposites. He's very reserved socially, but with me he talks freely, jokes, etc. He's ambitious. He's upset about the fact that I'm working, so he got a part-time job at a switchboard. He's going to be a high school teacher. He's a biology major. He's very conscientious. He wants to go to Europe." (How do you feel

Case V (Mrs. E)

about these plans?) "I feel that as long as he wants something that is at all reasonable I would go along. I think marriage should be that. He wouldn't do anything that wouldn't please me. There are many things we disagree about. I like suburban living, he would like to live in the country, where it's really private and isolated. We have a problem with clothes. He's more casual, I like to dress up more. When I get mad or I get in a disagreement, I let him know I'm mad, or I yell. He never argues. He refuses to raise his voice. Very strange. I'm the sort who, while I never have, could conceive of myself getting angry enough to throw a dish or something. He never would. He won't argue at all. He will quietly withdraw. He feels terrible about my working. I think it's silly of him to take that extra job. I want him to use his time for study, but he feels better." (Doesn't it limit the time he has available for you?) "Very definitely. It made me think I might just as well be working the four-to-twelve shift. I never see him; I hate being alone. When we're together it's extremely good. He's very affectionate and talks out his problems with me. He loves to discuss things, and I think we have a good marriage."

In this session one began to see the contradictions in her statements about her husband. Something was not quite as she stated it. She talked of her husband as being ambitious, yet except for her urging he would have settled willingly for non-skilled work. In the very first session she had said that the husband had quit college and returned only after marrying her. It is also indicative that she brought up her husband immediately after talking about her maternalistic relationship to the brother with whom she also fought a great deal. Associative linkage alone would make one suspect that she was quite maternalistic to her husband and was the dominant one in the family. One might also suspect that her description of her mother could well be a description of herself. The gratuitous remark that her mother never dominated the father suggests denial. All of this points to more dissatisfaction and conflict in the marriage than she was willing to admit to herself, let alone the interviewer.

The subject began the next session by discussing money, her attitudes about accepting money from her parents, who were quite generous, and her husband's contrasting attitude about this. This led quickly into the discussion of the conflict

55

between her and her husband. She contrasted her parents with her husband's parents.

"They [his parents] are very withdrawn. They never celebrate birthdays. I think my husband makes an issue of not accepting from my parents because he feels that casts a light on his parents. When my parents come they bring food, hampers, things of that sort. I don't mind. I appreciate it—it saves us money. I feel it's warm and friendly too. I'm confused— sometimes my husband talks me into the fact that it's too dependent, it's interfering. Then I feel he's right. We shouldn't accept it, and they shouldn't do it. On the other hand, I feel it's something they want to do, and it makes them feel good, and it makes me feel good. I don't have any trouble letting them know when I don't like things. I've told my mother off plenty of times. I've gotten angry very easily. It's not hard for me to express anger when I feel it. My husband is a stamp collector. He spends the whole day in the library with his stamps. He had a book report to do for school, and he didn't do it. I knew he had to do it. I came home from work and snapped at him when I realized that he'd been at the library but not studying. I came home with severe back pain I'd had the day before. I came home irritable, tired from work. I'd had a fight with a nurse and told her off, so I was irritable when I came in."

She then described another episode in which she had started quizzing her husband. He hedged, but she finally got him to the point where he admitted that he had not been studying but had been working on his stamps. "I yelled at him about the exams coming up. If I don't harp on it he won't study. I hate to leave things until the last minute. He tends to cram. Once we had our only real fight over this. He said he needs the tension to cram before he can study, but I'm afraid he'll get off the track again as he did before. He doesn't seem to get as upset about defeat as I do, but he's more withdrawn. I keep promising myself that I won't say anything to him, but then I start worrying. I worry about his future—he's so unsure. I know he quit once. Supposing he didn't want this? What could I do about it?" (What would you?) "I can't think of it. I know I'd probably make life miserable for him. I worry about finances and the future. He gives in to me an awful lot. I often thought that this is not what I wanted. I broke up with a fellow because he was always giving in to me. This annoys

56

me in a husband. I would rather he shows more strength. Before marriage, I always thought I wanted a man who was a strong man of the house, domineering but not intimidating." (How come you married your husband then?) "I don't know. I fell in love. I think maybe I saw him as a stronger person than he was before marriage." (It is difficult to believe you were deceived. You knew he was a gentle, permissive person before you married him, didn't you?) "Yes, I guess I really did. I don't know why I married him." (Could you get along with a domineering man?) "I don't know. I do like my own way pretty much. You know, really, when I think of it, it's pretty much like my parents. He tends to lean on me in the same way that my father did except with one difference—I make sure to leave the finances to him."

This session indicated how this subject repeated in her marriage the pattern of her mother and father. It confirmed some of the speculation of the early sessions about her domination of the husband. Her marriage repeats not only the parental pattern, but the sibling relationship as well. It also confirms the usual unreliability of answers to questions about life attitudes and goals. This subject, like almost all the unmarried nurses who were interviewed, wanted "a strong man I could lean on; one who could dominate me." At least this is what she consciously said and perhaps consciously believed. If one were to take her responses at face value, the information would have been grossly misleading. On the other hand, her unconscious fantasies and the pattern of her associations would have predicted, despite her verbalizations to the contrary, that she would marry a man she could handle. Confirmation of the degree to which her awareness of her husband's inadequacies affected her came from dreams of three different nights, which were reported in the next session.

In the first dream: "My husband and I were returning north after living in the tropics. It was so nice to see the ice and snow after so much time. Then I was in a bus, and somehow or other I was separated from my husband, and I was now going to visit him. I was driving along the frozen lake, and then the ice began to break up and people were drowning, and we just continued on our way." She had just seen *The King and I,* and it reminded her of the *Uncle Tom's Cabin* sequence in the movie, where the fleeing slave runs across the ice in an attempt to escape and join her husband.

In the second dream: "I was a nurse in a strict seclusion ward. I was tending a colored patient. A priest went in to see him. I was waiting, and then I found out that he had hung the priest."

The third dream "was like a movie scene. It wasn't the twentieth century. It was like primitive Russia. We were on horseback. We were wolf-hunting in terrain that wasn't too dissimilar from that near our home. We used a lamb as bait. It was a crude sport. When the wolves would come after the lamb we'd shoot them. Then we had a picnic and ate the wolf meat and berries, and then we all sat around and sang songs."

The first dream, in which she and her husband are returning from the tropics, with the separation on the ice, the breaking up of the ice, and the ignoring of the drowning people confirms her awareness of her estrangement from the husband. The equation of her husband with a Negro patient is another refutation of her consciously stated views. The hanging of the priest suggests a warning to the interviewer—that he is treading on dangerous ground. The trapping of the wolf with a lamb may indicate her feeling of having devoured one man (her husband) and presenting a warning to the other (the interviewer).

Many other attractive speculations might be made about the specific dream symbols, but since there were limited associations they remain only speculative. What does stand out is the subject's capacity for violent emotion and the extreme amount of rage and destructiveness beneath her surface composure.

Mrs. E makes an interesting contrast with Miss D. Both girls, so different in temperament, manner, and psychodynamics, were at the time of interviewing struggling with a very real, current problem—a crisis in their relationships with men.

Miss D was more controlled. Suppression and repression were her tools. Yet she exposed her problems with relatively little special maneuvering on the part of the interviewer. She was depressed and ready for unburdening. By catching contradictory implications in early sessions and constantly confronting her with these (i.e. her "desire to get married," the availability of a boy she "loved," and her unwillingness to marry) in an interview that was otherwise non-structured, a catharsis occurred. She exposed to the interviewer the affair

Case V (Mrs. E)

she had hidden from her friends and family, and revealed, perhaps for the first time even to herself, the degree to which she had outgrown her home-town sweetheart.

Mrs. E denied her problem by pretending her husband was the strong man she claimed to want, but the denial was flimsy and ineffectual. A relatively open, talkative individual—all that was required of the interviewer was to give her enough freedom and not constrict her associations—she soon reached a point where her true feelings came out.

Two different individuals with different defense structures and different dynamics, through a psychoanalytic approach, exposed current unhappiness in love: Miss D with a sense of relief; Mrs. E with a growing sense of anguish.

CASE VI

(Miss F)

Miss F was a twenty-three-year-old girl who looked much older. She was thin, drawn, and tense. While she was extremely articulate, with a degree of sophistication not found in the rest of the group, there was a note of irony and self-derision in her tone and a marked cynicism. She approached the interviews with more openness, more candor, and more exposure than do many patients in a first interview. She was willing and eager to have someone listen to her story.

Miss F demonstrates some of the difficulties encountered with a subject who, in a sense, is too ready to talk, presenting the danger of uncovering too much, too soon.

She started by giving her history. Her father had once been a very successful attorney. However, ever since Miss F could recall, he had been an alcoholic on a downhill course. For the past ten to twelve years his problem had been particularly acute, culminating in his losing his job. For the past seven years the family had been supported by public welfare. Miss F's life since early memory had been a gradual dissolution of

61

family assets, car, home, clothes, etc. Her father, still a young man, was now suffering from an alcoholic psychosis. She described her mother as gentle but weak. "If you can't lick them, join them. That's her motto." Her mother was fine as long as her father was, but for the past five to ten years, she, too, had been essentially an irresponsible alcoholic. At the age of twelve Miss F had the responsibility of the house, doing the cooking, shopping, etc., because of her mother's alcoholism. Nonetheless, she talked about her family with some affection and with great compassion. When questioned about whether she did not feel resentment or anger, she replied that she found it almost impossible to lose her temper, or show anger or hostility in any way.

Interestingly, she described herself as being like her mother, a very dependent person. Her self-image seemed a strange one for someone who since the age of twelve had run the household for two alcoholic parents. She was questioned on this point, and it became apparent that she was referring to suppressed dependency cravings for which, even in limited awareness, she had no tolerance. Characteristically in individuals deprived of the normal dependency gratifications of childhood, unconscious cravings grow and are maintained into adult life. The individual denies such needs, which seem impossible to gratify and "unworthy" of an adult, but in so denying is forced to "lean over backward" and suppress dependency gratifications that are perfectly appropriate and normal.

When the interviewer pointed out how completely *independent* she had been, how her whole life had been a history of people leaning on her, she became visibly upset and said, "Yes, I have these cravings, but there's no one to be dependent on." Spontaneously she went directly from that subject to a discussion of her relationships with men. The associative linkage was direct and meaningful. The relationships were a continuous horror story in which she had obviously sought men who could exploit her and use her, who were, at best, dependent and passive, and, at worst, manipulative and sadistic. She was seriously involved in four major romances. The first was with an older man in his mid-twenties, when she was sixteen. She was almost totally inexperienced sexually, and he exploited this. In her first contact she was taken by force in what constituted a near equivalent of rape. The affair lasted only the summer.

Case VI (Miss F)

The second major affair was with a student at college. This time dating led gradually to sexual relations. The boy was an overt schizophrenic. She became pregnant, but the boy refused to believe her, telling everybody that she was trying to force him into marriage. She was shocked by this reaction, broke off with him, and refused to see him again or tell him anything about the pregnancy. She confided in her parents. She knew nothing about abortion at that time and assumed the only choice open to her was to have the baby and give it away. She went to Florida, got herself a job, supported herself until the time of her delivery, and then turned the baby over to an agency. She told this with no self-pity, saying, "It wasn't a horrendous period." She worked hard and made friends, pretending to be married. The only desperate time was when she had to give the baby away.

The third affair was with a resident in the hospital. He claimed to love her. They were making plans for marriage. All of their friends knew she was engaged, so when she became pregnant, she was not unduly concerned. At a point of her pregnancy when abortion was no longer safe (by this time, being a nurse, she knew of its availability), she discovered by chance that her fiancé had a wife and children. She was forced again to go to a social-service agency to have her child. She told this with a great deal more pain than the first episode.

The next romance of any significance was a purely sexual affair with a married man who had five children. She knew "it would never go anywhere." She "never hoped or planned on anything coming out of it." She talked as though she had no right any more to ask anything of any man. The exploitative pattern of all these relationships, the inadequacies of the men, and her masochistic involvement seemed only too apparent. In addition, she had recently found that she had severe gynecological problems, and there was a question of whether she might not need a hysterectomy in the near future. "I'm twenty-three and feel like a woman of sixty." The interviewer asked her how she thought she always managed to get involved with the kind of man she did, and whether she thought it was purely chance. This led to a long catharsis about her own feelings of inadequacy, the sum of which was that she had no right to expect or aspire to anything. Feelings of unworthiness were quickly related back to childhood. For the first time in the interviews (and perhaps in her life) she poured forth

63

her sense of shame about her parents, her feeling of being cheated by them, her fear of bringing friends home, her sense of humiliation, and her resentment.

In the fourth session she related the following dream: "I was in my home town. I was with my roommate. We were going to a conference. It was very dark. I kept stumbling and bumping into things, not knowing where I was going, bumping into street poles and things. A friend came over—he felt the back of my neck and noticed I had enlarged lymph nodes. Then some hoodlums started chasing me—he was fighting with them. He was trying to save me. I became frantic, I was rushing about, looking for help. I went into the house to ask for help. The people in the house were calmly watching TV. I explained to them how desperate and critical the situation was and that they must come and help. They said they couldn't leave until the commercial came on. Then finally when we did get to the police, that was all wrapped up in red tape. They gave me the runaround, and I couldn't seem to get to someone who would actively help."

She related this to certain bizarre events over the weekend. She was without a date on Saturday night. A neighbor brought over a visiting Frenchman. He spoke little English, and communication was difficult. He seemed pleasant enough until her roommate and the neighbor left, whereupon he became sexually aggressive. At first she was merely annoyed—but his persistence came to the point of physical overpowering. She locked herself in the bathroom until he left. The panic subsided, and she began to think of her lonely state, her desire for love, and the kinds of affairs she had been involved in. She started crying and shaking uncontrollably. This ushered in a weekend of agitation, sobbing spells, and outbursts of rage totally inconsistent with her previous behavior.

For the first time in years of living with her roommate, she felt angry with her. A few friends called, and she screamed at them over the telephone. "This has never happened before," she said. "I have never lost control before." On Sunday, a girl friend called who had a history of severe emotional disturbance. She had been accustomed to calling regularly for support and reassurance. The subject had always responded by giving her a solicitous hearing. She was shocked to hear herself screaming over the telephone, "I've got my own problems and I don't have to listen to yours." She became ex-

Case VI (Miss F)

tremely upset at behaving like this. She felt that she was losing all control. She said: "For the entire weekend I was physically shaking like a leaf. I couldn't control my body."

Some of her specific associations with the dream were as follows: She was at the time on a cancer service; the enlarged lymph nodes meant that there was a tumor that had spread—it was a sign of hopelessness, of illness that could not be corrected. The emphasis she felt in the dream was that no one cared or was interested, since everyone was involved in their own lives and pleasures.

The dream exposes the subject's mounting panic. She is stumbling in the dark on the way to a conference—in all likelihood her feelings about the interviews and where they are leading. Her specific associations indicate her terror that she will be led to discover her condition is malignant. Her angers and resentment at the depriving world at large are being mobilized. She had kept this anger bottled up for many years and she was terrified of losing control, of being hurt. To show anger was, for her, to live in a world of violence, brutality, and attack, and she was totally unprepared for this. There was none of the sense of direction, guidance, and purpose that would accompany such exposure in a therapeutic situation. Miss F was aware of this. She said: "I feel I am being stirred up. I never usually snap back at my roommate. I'm beginning to feel that I shouldn't stir up something that I'm not going to finish. I was getting along well enough before."

Miss F reported that she had felt enormous release after the first few sessions, particularly after discussing her sexual history on Saturday. She left with a sense of elation. Then she said she did not have anyone with whom to share this feeling. It was as though there had been a certain degree of liberation, a certain recognition of the desire for love, and a readiness to admit others into her feeling, followed by an awareness that there was no one. Only with the interviewer could she share it. She had the feeling of "leaning" and being dependent on the interviewer, with the frightening realization that this was only a temporary relationship.

The interviewer devoted the last half of the fourth session and the fifth session to covering up some of the material that had previously come out and to discussing in a reassuring way the question of the girl's future, giving positive advice in terms of both job possibilities and the possibility of therapy. The interviewer emphasized that he would be available if she should ever want to go into therapy, or for any consultative purposes. She was extremely interested and ended the fourth session with the idea of going into therapy. Then with the reassurative nature of that session and the following session she became less involved, withdrawing into her original cynical pose. By the close of the fifth session, she had reverted to a somewhat slick, sardonic manner. When questioned on how she felt about the five sessions, she said she was extremely gratified and had enjoyed them. She was glad of the experience. She said it gave her food for thought, and she would not be at all surprised if she went into therapy in the near future. She felt that she would miss the sessions, that they were something she had come to look forward to, but that there was probably a certain sense of relief in ending them.

Miss F is not presented for the purpose of discussing her psychodynamic patterns or the methods used in eliciting them. Her spontaneous outpouring with little assistance from the interviewer was what one expects from a well-motivated, disturbed patient and therefore required no special interviewing techniques. It was precisely this point that created its own special problem.

Miss F's openness and candor led the interviewer to treat her as though she were a patient. The flow of her speech was so free and her associations so spontaneous that, almost by habit, the interviewer slipped into a therapeutic approach. The timing and nature of his questions and comments tended to open up problems, directing her toward further self-revelation. The interviewer engaged in psychosocial research must be careful to remember that the subject is not a patient in a continuing therapy, with all of the protections implied in that. There is a responsibility to the subject to permit him to maintain his illusions until such time as he himself may choose, or be forced, to face repressed feelings. The problem here is not eliciting information, but protecting the co-operating individual from premature insights.

(Miss G)

Miss G is presented to demonstrate the importance of transference phenomena even in a relationship as transient and limited as this.

Miss G was twenty-three years old, mildly plump, and round in the face. She smiled almost continuously during the early part of the sessions, and, in some peculiar way, in speech and manner, managed to give the impression of being middle-aged. One had the feeling that she quoted herself frequently and that she was determined to say, as well as to feel, the appropriate, socially acceptable thing.

Miss G presented her problems in terms either "of the way she used to be," or of problems that she saw in others, thus denying their existence in herself in the present. Nonetheless, her plumpness opened up one aspect of her problems. She said: "I was a problem eater till seven. I was picky and fussy about food. Then I gained a lot. I was always a little overweight when I grew up, but I never thought of it as being a great problem." (Why the change at seven?) "My brother is

67

six years younger. My mother didn't have time to fuss with me about eating." Significant among some of the facts of her background was her claim that she did not hold grudges and let out anger easily. She felt better after letting it out, she said, and she was "always square and right out in the open." The things that made her angry were injustices, people falsely accused, situations permitting righteous indignation.

She talked of her mother with great fondness, but said that she and her mother used to fight a great deal. Again she used the past tense. Miss G felt that she had given her whole history in the first ten minutes. Having crisply listed all the facts about herself and saying she had no problems, she sat back and remarked that that was it.

In the first session the interviewer encouraged her with a few questions. In the second session however he indicated that he was going to be primarily a listener. (You know that I am interested in you as a whole, so that anything you say is relevant. I want you to talk.) Miss G blocked, and there was a long pause. "For the first time in my life I am at a loss for words." Again a long pause. Miss G blushed profusely. "This is terrible." Long pause again. (Just say anything.) Long pause. "I'll talk about my roommate. I like her, but underneath I think there may be resentment. I like to be praised when I do a good job. There are certain things about my roommate that I don't like. I don't tell her about these. I tell her things that I like about her. If I told her, I think she'd change." Miss G then went on to talk about other things and returned to her roommate and said: "She's very different. I'm always ready to go and do. She's cautious, always putting on the brakes, worrying, etc. For example, I used to go skiing; she said it's dangerous. 'You might break your leg.' Now she produced a hesitancy on my part. I'm a little frightened. I accepted a blind date. My roommate said: 'You don't even know him.' By the time I went out with him she had talked me into being frightened. She didn't even go home on Christmas Eve. She only had the night off. I would have gone home, hell or water, even if I had only a few hours and had to travel twenty-four hours to do it."

Here she was using her roommate as a comparison with, and also, one suspects, a projection of, certain of her own denied fears. She warned the interviewer that she needed praise, suppressed hostility, and was more fearful than she

68

would admit. So, while ostensibly discussing her roommate, she was exposing herself. Gradually, however, the talk became more exclusively about the unique and very specific problems of the roommate. After ten or fifteen minutes of this, the interviewer challenged her. (What do you think about the selection of subjects you have chosen to talk about?) "Does it mean how important my roommate is in my life?" (Perhaps. What else could it mean?) "I don't know." (Well, think about it.) Long pause. "You think I'm avoiding talking about myself." The interviewer nodded. "It seems that way, but I'm not at all aware of it. You told me, anything that comes to my mind. I'm usually quite frank and open. I know my standards, yet I don't condemn other standards." Immediately then Miss G went into a discussion of the sexual life of her friends, mentioning those who got pregnant. For the first time she then discussed some of her own personal sexual feelings. She felt that she enjoyed sex and had to exercise self-control because she was frightened of pregnancy.

The immediate shifting to a sexual subject on being challenged about her evasion, has of course, a degree of significance, but what seemed most interesting about Miss G was her response to the particular challenge, which seemed quite gentle. After some brief preliminaries in the following session, she got around to the previous session. "I think I got a little annoyed. I'm terribly tired with this new schedule I'm on. That day was exhausting because it was the day that I had switched schedules from day to night, and I had no sleep. I really didn't want to come to see you at all (she blushed) and then when I came I talked about the wrong thing." (Did you feel criticized by me?) "I felt, why didn't you stop me. I spent twenty minutes talking about the wrong thing. I didn't really think it was the wrong thing. I felt it was important to know her. I think if you know her, it helps to know me, since I am a friend of hers. I wasn't mad, certainly not enough to say anything." This was all said with mounting anger and show of emotion. "I felt very noble coming after the double shift. Instead of getting praise, I got criticism. I feel I volunteered to tell, and I was disturbed that maybe you thought I was being evasive. I felt somehow or other exposed in all of this. It reminded me of when my father died. I was age eleven. I decided I wasn't going to cry. If something really bothers me I don't like to show it. I *hate* to let other people know that they

69

can get me that mad. (This with a marked degree of animation.) I always felt I could talk well and prided myself about the way I took criticism. I always give the appearance to others that I take criticism well and that nothing bothers me." (Obviously you are very sensitive to criticism.) "I'm terribly sensitive. Nobody knows that. I'm thought of as a jolly sort that's unruffable. I blushed in here two or three times. I've never done that before, and in so doing I showed that I'm sensitive to criticism, and I felt I let you know something no one else knows about me." (Why is it that important that they should not know that about you?) "I think of it as a weakness of character. If I cook something for my roommate and she doesn't praise it, that bothers me." (So you were bothered when I didn't praise you for coming here after your double shift, which was a sacrifice on your part, but rather said what to you was a criticism.) "Yes, I'm sure it comes from my mother. She never praised. Now she does. She learned from my brother who is six years younger. My brother just doesn't take it. My mother always tended to show our deficits rather than our strengths. She didn't want us to be spoiled. She had a hard job raising us. She was a lab technician and a bank clerk. My father died at the age of thirty-four of a coronary. Her one real fault was this lack of praising."

This led into the first detailed discussion of her mother and her background in a way that was not stereotyped, in which she revealed the degree of conflict. Her mother was extremely interested in her, managing to work, to support the family, and still to maintain the typical maternal involvement with school activities. However, she was even more involved with the younger brother. The brother demanded more and got it. Miss G didn't seem to be able to demand. An example of the sort of material she presented is the following quotation: "I was really defiant. Part of it was that everybody felt my mother was so great that it didn't give me much room to be angry. She was very free with me. When the other parents set time limits, she set no time limits. At that time I thought I was being put upon." This girl with her working mother obviously wanted controls and direction, even if it were in the matter of disciplining. She took her relative freedom as a sign of less interest than the more directed approach to the younger child in the family.

Miss G was a basically well-integrated young woman who,

while quite guarded and determined to make a good impression, managed nonetheless to reveal many of her psychodynamic patterns and basic defense mechanisms. The way in which they were exposed is of particular interest.

Miss G's mother was so patient, understanding, and self-sacrificing that directing anger toward her became difficult. To avoid guilt for her hostility, it was necessary for Miss G to feel wounded and misunderstood. Since her mother's chief fault was a tendency to withhold praise and point out defects, Miss G cultivated righteous indignation. When the interviewer "criticized" her rather than praising her for her effort, he committed the characteristic offense of her mother, and in true transference style the response exposed the first real show of emotion. The dramatic change in her behavior was a transference response and reveals its potential value in even these brief relationships.

CASE VIII

(Miss H)

Miss H was a slender, moderately pretty girl of twenty-two. The very first comment written by the interviewer was his impression of her as an obedient little girl, and it proved to be prophetic. Miss H cultivated and exploited the little-girl role. It colored most of her adaptive maneuvers. The presentation of her case will focus on this dominant psychodynamic pattern.

Miss H had difficulty with free-associating from the start. When she did get going, she immediately got onto a current problem, a love affair which had reached an obstacle because of a difference in religion. Miss H is Roman Catholic, and the boy was a Protestant who couldn't accept her Catholicism. She said she was torn between loyalty to her religion and affection for the boy. They had been going together for a year, and he had just left town. She wasn't sure which direction this relationship would go. He called her regularly, and she was hoping that he would ask her to marry him. By the end of the fifth hour the interviewer, at least, had no doubt that she knew exactly where she was going in her relationship with this boy and that he was no match for her. The interesting thing about her presentation was that, while appearing quite stilted, she also seemed extremely frank. She volunteered nothing except trivia. But when asked questions, even of the most personal nature, she went into the most intimate details of her life without hesitation. She seemed to give everything, but only on direct "order." Here again was the "obedient little girl."

In the first session, she recalled two dreams she had had some time before: "I was walking down a dark cellar stair. There were all these cats around me. They jumped on my back. They were clawing into me. My boy friend was way ahead. I screamed, 'Don't leave me, get them off me.'" Although the subject was incapable of associating to this dream, the interviewer felt it reflected a certain degree of latent hostility to women, with a fear of abandonment by a man.

In the second dream: "I was in a concentration camp. I was forced to submit to sexual intercourse with a handsome German soldier. I was very aroused and enjoyed it very much." To this the patient associated smilingly and stated that probably this was the only way she could admit that she wanted sex.

In exploring her relationship with her boy friend, she revealed that while she was extremely naïve sexually, she had had sexual intercourse with him a week before he left town. She did not seem to regret it or feel upset about it. One had the sense that she was pleased and that she would use it, and the boy's guilt about it, as a hold on him. She even said that she had been hoping that her boy friend would make a sexual move long before he did. "He didn't have to press me—I decided that I wanted it. I had decided long before, and I think it was really I who made the decision." (You're a girl who knows what you want.) Unhesitatingly Miss H responded, "Yes. My parents didn't want me to come to New York, but I'm here. They didn't want me to leave home, but I managed it," etc.

The next session again saw her extremely blocked, for a reason that came out somewhat later. It was an agonizing session for her, and she could find very little to talk about. Then she seemed spontaneously to find a way out of her problems. She mentioned a patient on the ward with a specific surgical problem and realized she had a subject she could get her teeth into and talk about for hours. She thus found in her way the same defensive maneuver utilized by Miss F (Case VI). This was a way out of her dilemma. By talking about other people, she could still be a good girl, saying what came to mind, but making sure that what came to mind was safe. The extreme blockage at this point was probably due to the success of the interviewer in eliciting information in the first hour or two. Because of the need for overt obedience, Miss H answered intimate details about her sexual life for which she really was unprepared emotionally. At that point, being a good girl was a more necessary security maneuver than was protecting her self-image. It produced anger and caution and the kind of subtle passive defiance that she had utilized from childhood. The solution was to talk—but only about patients. The colloquy that followed—direct challenge of this defense—proved to be the most interesting part of her sessions.

The interviewer permitted her to talk about patients for about twenty minutes, then broke in. (It's a lot easier to talk about other persons' problems than your own, isn't it?) "Yes, that's right, but if you don't like what I choose to talk about when I select the subject, why don't you ask questions?" (No, I think we'll continue to try this method of letting you pick the subject.) "I'm not a person who volunteers information readily." (You don't like talking about yourself.) "No, I don't. I'm good at small talk but not about myself." (Why not?) "I don't think people are interested." (I am.) "I don't believe you." (Why not?) "If I get too close to anyone I feel I'll get hurt. I can't prove this statement, it's a feeling I have. If someone I'm close to gets angry with me, I get more hurt. I don't seem to get angry, I get frightened. I have often felt that if I went off the deep end, I'd be one of those 'schizies' that don't let anyone into their real little world."

This had come as a spontaneous burst of information from the patient. Then, almost as though recognizing that she had revealed something of herself, she returned to intellectualizing and started talking about schizophrenia as a disease and of her experience with it in psychiatry. Again the direct challenge produced results with her, although the nature of the result in this case was somewhat disturbing.

Even when Miss H thought she was revealing very little and tried to be defensive, she managed to expose herself through her defenses. For example, she decided another safe way of associating was to talk about furnishing her apartment. With all the objects in the apartment she had found it necessary to shop for—which she described in some detail —she could not avoid constantly referring back to the curtains she needed for her windows, which in turn led back to some mention of her need for privacy. The patient was unquestionably unaware that, at the same time she was guarding against exposure, she was revealing that she was guarding against exposure. While she might protect her privacy in every indirect way, when confronted directly by an authority figure she must be obedient. The need to be the obedient child always took precedence. The nature of her psychodynamics determined not only what she would and would not tell, but how she would tell and how she would not tell. The following final confrontation seemed to confirm explicitly much that had been said before.

She had been describing her mother and father as easygoing, "adorable" stereotypes, yet she had previously said that she had not been able ever to talk freely to them. The interviewer asked her how she explained the fact that, since they were such "adorable" people, she couldn't talk with them.

"I don't know, I always have seen myself as outgoing and uninhibited." (That's strange. Do you think you've been uninhibited with me?) "No, I guess I haven't." (How come?) "Well, the only thing I'm inhibited about is my own personal feelings." She then went on to say that what she meant by being uninhibited was that she felt free to take off her shoes in public, to do "kooky" things, etc. Then she seemed concerned that the interviewer might be implying that she hadn't given him what he wanted. This was extremely disturbing to her, as might be expected. She said: "I really don't know what you want from me. When I ask, and I certainly ask enough, all you say is that you want everything. I felt last week that I was holding back, but I couldn't say what. I really didn't know. I guess I just don't want you to see me—I don't want to talk. I usually feel good when I get out of here, especially after the first session. I told you about my affair—you didn't criticize me. I did feel guilty about it. I was sure I would never tell anybody about it. I was shocked to find myself telling you. I don't know how you got me to tell you. There was something about that matter-of-fact attitude of yours—the way

76

Case VIII (Miss H)

you just simply came out and asked it—as though you had a right to know. I was so shocked that you just came out and asked it—it was so personal." (Why then did you answer?) "Because you asked me. I was stunned. People don't normally do that. Then I felt such enormous sense of relief, unloading, almost gratitude, that I had told someone about him."

She answered because she was asked. Indeed, consistent with the psychodynamic picture of this girl, one had the feeling that if one only knew all the specific questions to ask, there would be nothing that she wouldn't answer. Obedience to direct command of an authority figure was essential. While maintaining the air of obedience, however, there would be independent action and a stubborn self-will exercised via manipulation and passive aggression. Defiance would always be indirect under the cover of apparent compliance.[1]

[1] Subsequent evaluation of the psychological tests and reevaluation of the interviews themselves led to the conclusion that certain aspects of this girl's pathology had been overlooked by the interviewer. The interested reader is referred to pp. 100–1.

(Miss I)

Miss I was a tall, blond, pretty girl whose good looks were somewhat marred by a bad complexion. She had a gentle, but not shy, manner and smiled frequently. Miss I was quite co-operative and talked reasonably freely. There was no hostile defiance as was seen in some of the other nurses. One sensed that she honestly wanted to co-operate, and in the first hour she revealed a great deal of information about her background, the facts of her life, her attitudes, aspirations, etc. She talked quite freely for the whole hour with little prompting. Somehow, however, it was all two-dimensional. There was an absence of any clear-cut picture of unconscious trends and psychodynamic patterns. Perhaps the most interesting special aspect of this case occurred in the second and third hours and illustrates a potential pitfall in cases of this sort. The interviewer's impatience probably led him to press prematurely for information.

The subject started the second session by asking the interviewer to ask her a question. (I'm interested in you as a person, so I'm interested in everything about you. I leave it up to you. What do you think I should know?) "I guess you should know my feelings, feelings about things that concern me." The interviewer agreed, stating that she had not discussed her feelings at all. She then proceeded to discuss her feelings about being a nurse. These were more accurately her ideas. She talked about nurses in general and then dating in general. At this point the interviewer decided to get specific with her. In response to specific questions about her dating, Miss I gave a very specific, honest, non-evasive answer, so that the interviewer found himself asking her about her sexual relations with men and whether she had had intercourse with her boy friend (she had never had intercourse), some of the reasons why she would or would not, when she might, etc. In what seemed like a free-and-easy, though stilted, manner, she answered these questions. However, she returned to the third session with the following two dreams:

"Three men broke into my apartment. I was at the table, eating. I was frightened. They came to rob me. I was relieved when all they took was a bottle of milk.

"I was sitting in the bathtub, taking a bath. Jim was sitting in a window trying to look in. I was shifting positions so as not to expose myself or be seen."

She was quite blocked in this session and found difficulty talking about the dreams. The blocking had been growing ever since the first session, but this was more extreme than usual. When asked about Jim, she laughed. "He's a brother-in-law of a very good friend. He's a real joker. It's the kind of thing he would do." She described him as an alcoholic, charming and ingratiating. "He's one of the raunchiest (evidently slang for sexy or, more accurately, sexual) people I know. He's always making funny, vulgar comments, but he gets away with it for some reason because of his pleasant manner. They never seem to be offensive."

At this point the interviewer abstracted the dream in the following way: The dream is about someone trying to look in on you and see you in your most private moments, and you're trying to shift position and avoid exposure. (What do you think this can refer to?) Miss I answered: "I have no idea. It doesn't seem to relate to anything I can think of." After more blocking and avoidance by the subject, the interviewer took the initiative and interpreted this as her response to the previous session, particularly to the fact of being questioned about her sexual life. "That's very interesting," she said. (Well, interesting or not, do you think there's any truth to it?) "I don't know. I suppose I've been somewhat hesitant. I've never had any therapy, so I'm not sure exactly what you're supposed to do. I certainly feel comfortable with you. Still, I must admit, there's a certain hesitancy about certain things. Like even telling you the dreams. It seems too personal. I don't know whether to tell you. My roommate says: 'You're not going to tell him *that*.' It's sort of embarrassing to talk about being in the bathtub." (Why did you tell me?) "I felt, what's the good of a research if you're not going to co-operate. If I'm giving this much time to it, it seems a little stupid not to do it the right way. I've been trying to be co-operative and trying to think of what my worries are so that I could tell you, but I honestly don't think I have any."

The dreams expose her response to this invasion of her privacy. First there is the reassurance of the first dream—a denial of the anxiety and a desexualization. Then the second dream reveals her need to conceal, perhaps her wish to reveal, but, in any case, her determination to cover up. The shifting of positions in the dream might have an even more specific meaning in indicating a characteristic defensive pattern. Certainly, the last two sessions were characterized by a light "shifting" from one non-revealing subject to another.

Miss I represented to her interviewer his least satisfactory case. It may be that there was less beneath the surface than the interviewer imagined. On the other hand, there is no question that the directness of questioning about sexual behavior was somewhat shocking to a girl of her naïveté. Whether she would have exposed more of her dynamics if not threatened so early with questions about her sex life is a moot question, but one that has to be considered. Such timing is particularly critical in interviewing with limited hours.

CASE X

(Miss J)

Miss J was an attractive twenty-two-year-old girl of medium height and a good figure, although she made it clear that she had to watch her weight carefully. She discussed many seemingly disparate themes during the sessions: her mother's mental illness, the possibility of marrying her boy friend, her concern with money, and her weight. Of particular interest was the gradual way in which the relationship of these themes became clear and meaningful.

In the second session she described her boy friend: "He is a doctor. He's fairly wealthy in his own right. This bothers me." (It bothers you?) "I'd hate someone to say I love him for his money. I ask myself that. He can take off a week skiing; he has his own boat. Right now we've been going skiing for a couple of weeks. He says he'll teach me. I always become part of the boy I'm interested in and his interests. There was a boy in high school who had hot rods. I knew all about cars. Now I begin to worry with Tom, that I love him for his money." (Could you tell me more about your feelings for

83

him?) "Well, I'm overwhelmed. I'm a Scotch shopper.
Roger spent more on me. Taught me to respect money. Tom
wastes money. It's often nice to be able to just go to a movie you'd
like to see. I often date poor fellows. The debutante set is
boring, makes me feel uncomfortable. At R (her high school)
the wealthy girls drove up in convertibles. I felt inferior.
However, in school we all wore uniforms. Intellectually I was
their equal or better."

In session three: "I used to be very heavy till I was seven-
teen or eighteen, 175 pounds. The year before I went into
training—my family doctor gave me pills and I lost weight. I
now weigh 134. I go up to 144, I diet. I go on a diet for months
and then go off it, but I always watch my weight. When you're
so heavy your peer group is more critical than any other. I'm
still self-conscious with a group my own age. I still can feel
fat and ugly. I feel if I turn my back, they'd feel I have an
enormous behind. The smaller I am the more confident I feel.
My mother is the same. My father can eat thousands of
calories and not get heavy."

When the subject was thirteen, her mother had developed
a paranoid psychosis and never fully recovered. Before her
breakdown she had been extremely lively and outgoing. The
subject described her mother as a very free spender, both for
herself and for the family, and in discussing her parents she
said: "They never quarreled. Occasionally they quarreled
about my mother spending money.

"We are alike, my mother and I. She had ten brothers and
sisters. All ten became depressed. Three still are in a mental
institution. She had a horrible childhood. I wonder about a
congenital weakness. She was sort of manic-y before. She
can be suspicious with people and think my father and I are
trying to kill her. Her psychiatrist said she developed feelings
of inadequacy when her fertility was lost. I think she worried
that my father would be unfaithful. Some day I feel it could
happen to me. When I'm heavy, I feel no attractiveness and
no way of holding anyone."

Further remarks regarding money ran through the sessions.
Concerning the possibility of marrying her boy friend: "I'd
have to pay for my own wedding, so I'll wait," or, "I don't
feel I'm selfish. You hear about an only child being spoiled.
I don't feel I am. I have sound ideas about a dollar. I'm not
a money waster. I'm grateful for the things I have." Also, "I

CASE XII

(Miss L)

Miss L was a dark, attractive girl of twenty-five, and the set of her eyes gave her a slightly oriental look. Though she made good contact, seemed alert and intelligent, and had some spirit in her conversation, the interviews with her were among the least satisfactory of those done. It may be of value to discuss her from just this standpoint.

She described herself as "compulsive" and this was borne out by the way she told her story. It was factual and detailed, but despite her liveliness and alertness there was little free flow of emotion. She revealed exactly as much as she intended to or felt was appropriate, and she was not a person who forgot herself easily.

It was not a matter of her failure to indicate any problems. She made it clear that she was dissatisfied and felt bored and unfulfilled with nursing, and it was clear that she had great uncertainty as to what she wanted to do with her life. She was extremely fault-finding with the one man she felt she had been in love with and suspected she would have this tendency with other men as well.

89

Nor was there an absence of significant historical data. Her father, whom she appeared to romanticize, died when she was three. She and her mother had been "pals," and in the most revealing session in the interviews it turned out that she felt her mother had probably been too much of a "pal" and not enough of a protective figure. She had combined a feuding and a seductive relationship with her stepfather whom her mother had married when she was eight.

Most of the dissatisfaction with the sessions stemmed from the fact she was seldom spontaneous in her reactions. When she was eventually challenged on this, her answer was revealing: "Well, I've covered my life as far as the things I've been doing and seeing." (As far as the things you have been *doing* and *seeing,* yes.) She laughed and said: "I don't reveal myself. Underneath I can get hurt easily, and I don't show it. Outwardly I'm independent. If someone is kind to me I can be kind or loving back. I have to be shown first. I'm not the instigator. It's not that I'm shy or reserved. Many nurses on duty flirt with the doctors. People I work with, I'm professional with. I try to keep work professional. I don't joke around. In the cafeteria it's different. A doctor you work with and you go out with, it's harder to relax with than a doctor you don't work with. I'm a loner. I enjoy company when I choose it, not when it's forced upon me. I don't have any great mood swings. I'm far from calling myself unhappy. At present I'd prefer a somewhat more active social life. Partly it has been interfered with by the fact that I have been away on vacation so much. I'd like to start going out again."

Many times in the course of the interview she alluded to the fact that she had been very popular, but that at the time she was not going out as much as she would have liked. At times she appeared to be hinting that she was available, but that the interviewer would have to take more initiative.

Spontaneous emotional reactions are as important as dreams and free associations in psychodynamic investigation. With this girl one had the impression that even were she in therapy it would take a good deal of time to get past her well-integrated obsessional defenses. There is the possibility that more challenging of these defenses would have been productive, but it is perhaps more likely that she illustrates one limitation of the five-interview procedure when dealing with a subject of this sort.

Discussion, Conclusions, Applications

Discussion

Since this was a pilot study, an attempt was made to experiment slightly with the interviewing approach, although always within the confines of the psychoanalytic interview. Several of the girls were deliberately given some direction in the first few sessions and were led gradually into the unstructured procedure, while others were given free rein from the onset. Leaving the subject on her own, right from the beginning, proved to be definitely more productive. The girls would have preferred more questions and often made this clear, but they revealed much more without them. Their spontaneous associations were so informative that when eventually the interviewer wished to ask questions, the questions could be more specifically and intelligently framed. This also fit in with the interviewers' desire to finish up with a more directed and structured procedure and to use the last session to relieve anxieties that had been stirred up in the earlier sessions.

As has been indicated, when any basic defensive maneuvers

93

were interfering with communication, these had to be pointed out. Illustrations have been given of the more strenuous challenging that was occasionally necessary. The subjects' trend of associations, dreams, omissions, transference reactions—all tools that the analyst is geared to work with—were the most productive sources of information. To interpret such data properly, the interviewer must have a thorough knowledge of psychoanalytic theory as well as sufficient self-insight to avoid distortions of the data based on his own subjective reactions.

Since the subjects were not patients, some natural questions arose as to their motivation for participating in the project and revealing so much about their personal lives. They were originally asked to participate in a research project that was "a study of nurses." While non-psychiatric nurses who had never had any prior contact with the interviewers were chosen deliberately, it is certainly possible that nurses in general may have a willingness to co-operate with doctors that office workers, for example, would not have. As one observes the idiosyncratic way in which transference operated with different nurses, however, one is impressed with its intensity and the personal nature of its motivation, supporting the impression that it is not primarily a function of the fact that the subjects were nurses.

It is worth noting that the girls had no idea they would be going into their lives to the degree they eventually did. As it turned out, some of them clearly welcomed the opportunity to discuss themselves and their problems. Several made clear in various ways their distaste for the sessions and tried to reveal as little as possible. The advantage of the technique employed was that a great deal was learned even from such subjects. There is every reason to assume that the same would be true even with only partially co-operative subjects who were not nurses. The only important difficulty might come if significant numbers of any group refused to participate.

How much of a motivating factor was the money the subject received? Almost all of the original larger group of forty nurses had made clear their willingness to co-operate before receiving payment for their time was mentioned. It is possible, however, that once having begun, the money was a factor in persuading them to continue, although the authors' impression was that they would have completed the interviews without it. In related work done in Sweden,[1] Hendin was able to arrange for the Swedish nurses to be given time off from work for the interviews rather than paid for their participation, and this in no way interfered with their co-operation.

[1] Herbert Hendin, *Suicide and Scandinavia,* Doubleday Anchor, 1965.

Psychological Testing

Each nurse selected to be interviewed was also given a battery of psychological tests, which were evaluated independently of the interview material. The tests included the Rorschach, Thematic Apperception Test (TAT), Sentence Completion Test (SCT), Draw-a-Person and Bender-Gestalt. The selection of the tests, their administration, and original interpretation were the responsibility of the psychologist at the hospital. To protect the anonymity of the nurses and the hospital, this psychologist cannot, unfortunately, be credited.

While the study was not designed to evaluate the two methodologies, it was felt that a comparison of the results could prove illuminating. With this in mind, the data from both were presented to another psychologist, one of the present authors.

In the absence of the establishment of reliability of interpretation and without final validating criteria, any minute comparison of the two sources of inference would not be in order. Nor is the picture that emerged of any particular nurse

96

of primary importance. The two procedures, however, produced intriguing contrasts and similarities, and a few generalizations appear relevant:

1. In numerous instances, there appeared to be complete agreement on extremely subtle distinctions made independently by interviewer and tester. Even with an extremely guarded individual (Miss L), who managed to restrict her emotional involvement in interview and test situation alike, there was confirming evidence in both procedures of the role the early loss of her father had played in the psychogenesis of her present difficulties with men.

The interviewer's report on another nurse (Miss G) states, "One had the feeling that she quoted herself freely and that she was determined to say, as well as to feel, the appropriate, socially acceptable thing." Interesting confirmatory evidence was provided by the Rorschach record of this nurse in that the number of conventional (so-called "popular") responses constituted 90 per cent of the total, reflecting an unusual degree of overconventionality in thought processes.

In another instance (Miss F), both sources of information stress the difficulty the subject has with her dependency needs, in spite of the fact that in her behavior she has always been a "giver." In the first interview, the interviewer commented that the subject's dependent self-image probably represented only an apparent contradiction with her actual independent behavior. Subsequent interview material and excessive oral content in Rorschach responses corroborated this early view.

In the case of the tremendously overweight nurse (Miss C), both interviewer and psychologist agreed on the underlying ego weakness and stressed the use of denial as a major defense. Thus, although the subject was shown on the Rorschach test to be immobilized by her anxiety, the SCT indicates gross denial: MY NERVES "are no problem" and THE ONLY TROUBLE "is my weight."

In the cases of Miss J, Miss B, Miss L, Miss A, Miss I and Mrs. E, interviewer and psychologist agree on the subject's strong need to control and dominate. For example, Miss A, who managed to control her fiancé and subdue his sexual passion during a three-year engagement, related dramatically correlating TAT stories in which the woman's role was to quiet and calm the man in regard to both sex and aggression.

2. In other instances, interpretations from one source of data were enriched and clarified by data from the other source. For example, the interviews revealed how one nurse (Miss J), was apparently considering marrying a doctor for spurious reasons having to do with both his wealth and prestige. It was interesting to note that the figure-drawings of this nurse were the only ones in which the woman was drawn in a nurse's uniform and the male in a doctor's uniform, leading to the inference that she was highly dependent upon status symbols.

The psychologist summarized one nurse (Miss F) as "preferring a nurturing role where she can be mothering but at the same time resenting those who accept her in this way." Her reported history dramatized the manifestations of this need in her relationships with alcoholic parents, absconding males, and illegitimate babies. Such specifics obviously enrich our understanding of the subject's actual functioning. How pallid seem any of our generalizations or abstractions, related to the "Oedipus complex," "repressed hostility," "castration fear," "dependency needs," etc., when compared to their behavioral manifestations apparent in the actual life history! Nevertheless, a generalization or abstraction inferred from one source of data may help predict, clarify, organize, or give meaning to data from another source. The interviewers and the psychologists were particularly impressed by how frequently TAT Card 5 (a woman looking into a room through a half-opened door) elicited stories that obviously recapitulated the subject's attitudes toward the testing psychologist, who was a woman, and, on occasion, toward the interviewers as well.[2] Such attitudes ranged from a feeling of satisfaction at successful concealment to one of extreme indignation because of exposure. Miss F, for example, although initially a co-operative subject, revealed the extent of her anger and resentment, which later became apparent in interviewing, by the story she made up in response to TAT Card 5:

" 'Is there anybody home?' The nosy old lady from down the

[2] Although not usually considered the "transference" card for the usual doctor-patient relationship, data suggested the possibility that when the doctor's role is investigative rather than therapeutic, Card 5 may serve as a better stimulus for eliciting projections of transference attitudes than Card 12M (an older man leaning over a figure on a couch), which is usually assumed to have such "pull."

hall has stopped by to find out if there is any good gossip available. She is very perturbed because this housewife is out. She stays home a good deal of the time and expects other people like this housewife to be there to entertain her and provide her with any news of scandal which is her sustenance. She will see if there is anything interestingly about, like a letter from someone she knows, and then go back to her room to try again later."

3. In still other instances, what appear to be contradictions between test and interview data can be rationalized as merely different aspects of the same underlying problem. For example, on the basis of the Rorschach test of one girl (Miss D), the testing psychologist inferred that, "She is quite exhibitionistic and enjoys being in the limelight," although the interviewer had emphasized her "shyness." In spite of the apparent discrepancy, such dissimilar aspects of overt behavior may actually be dynamically related and motivationally similar. There is, in fact, ample evidence in both sources of data to indicate that Miss D may indeed be both "shy" and "exhibitionistic," and that both aspects of her behavior are a function of the same underlying impulses and her defense against them.

4. There are other discrepancies, however, that cannot be so discounted, particularly those related to the individual nurse's basic ego strength or ego integration (Miss A, Miss B, Miss H). In the absence of any final criterion, such differences are difficult to resolve. In reviewing the over-all data it appears that these differences were due primarily to errors of interpretation rather than to any inherent limitation of the data itself.

For example, in the case of one girl (Miss A), while the interview data supported the impression of a "paranoid integration," the psychologist's report made no mention of paranoid features and, on the whole, presented a much more healthy-appearing picture. In this particular instance, the subject's compliant, agreeable behavior apparently led the psychologist to underestimate her difficulties. The psychologist reported, "She is at ease in her feminine identification and unafraid of masculinity so that her relationships with both sexes appear warmly satisfying to her."

In discussion, the psychologist indicated that the basis for this inference was the subject's response to the Rorschach test in terms of the subject's willingness to identify Card VI as the male genital. Inspection of the test data revealed the following response, "Well, I'm sorry but I can't see anything but a male." In later questioning, she had added, "I can't see a male in there—just the genital organ." As an additional response, she then said, "And don't ask me why, but it reminds me of a thermometer too."

On examination, this response sequence indicates anything but "an ease in feminine identification." At the lowest level of inference, it would seem to suggest an overconcern and preoccupation with the male sex organ. More hypothetically, the response alternative might also imply the need to control the male, compensation for the lack of a phallus, oral or anal associations to sex, or the equation of sex with sickness. It is relevant to note that this girl's free associations during interviews showed marked concern with the violation of bodily integrity, including a traumatic episode involving the taking of rectal temperature and such dreams as being threatened by her fiancé with a penknife.

In another instance, it appears that the error was on the part of the interviewer. In the case of Miss H, the psychologist inferred much more pathology than that suggested by the interviewer. In reviewing the data, it seems evident that the interview material itself supports the psychologist's conclusions. For example, the interviewer commented on the fact that the subject volunteered only trivia, but when asked questions went without hesitation into the most intimate details of her life. In the first session, she had discussed her first sexual experience, which had occurred the previous week. Her reported dreams appeared to reflect great anxiety. She related her first dream as follows: "I was walking down a dark cellar stair. There were all these cats around me. They jumped on my back. They were clawing into me. My boy friend was way ahead. I screamed, 'Don't leave me, get them off me.'" To this dream, she was "incapable of associating." At the time, the interviewer related both the subject's frequent blocking and her numerous inconsistencies to her desire to play her role of obedient little girl.

On Card II of the Rorschach, she had responded, "Two elephants joining trunks and their knees have hit together causing blood to fall . . . shape sort of a deformed elephant." Her view that "I should have been a boy" supported the assumption that the phallic (deformed) elephant percept reflected other aspects of her self-image, as well as her fear of injury from close interpersonal contact. The one time the interviewer had challenged her obedient defenses she actually gave similar evidence of emotional pathology: "If I get too close to anyone I feel I'll get hurt . . ." She had then gone on to link involvement with a fear of going "off the deep end" and becoming psychotic.

In retrospect it seemed that the interviewer had ignored the negative implications of interview data, stressing the strength in this girl who "knew exactly where she was going in her relationship with this boy and that he was no match for her." In view of the fact that the interviewer changed techniques to no avail, one might wonder if the subject were not better able to control the interviewer than she was to control her boy friend, who was seemingly giving no evidence of returning from the distant city where he went shortly after having seduced her. In any event, the subject was not so sure of herself as the interviewer implied. On the SCT, she indicated: MY GREATEST FEAR "is living the rest of life alone"; I SUFFER "from loneliness quite often"; I SECRETLY "wish I were a gypsy."

In the last example the testing was more successful than the interviewing. In most of the other cases the interviewing gave a fuller and richer picture of the subject. However, errors of inference will probably always occur in interviewing as well as in testing. The training, experience, and skill of the psychologist will be major factors in minimizing test errors; the training, experience, and skill of the psychoanalyst will be major factors in minimizing errors in the interviews.

While it appears evident that interviewing could be used in future research without the support of testing, a collaborative effort in which interview and test material were compared and discussed during the course of the work would further minimize errors. Discrepancies could then be resolved through further exploration. In the present study, which was designed to test the applicability of a psychoanalytic approach to interviewing non-patients, it was naturally desirable to have the testing done separately. In future applications of analytic interviewing combined with testing, it should not be necessary to be specially concerned with the independent nature of the interviewer's conclusions.

Conclusions and Applications

If the procedure used with the nurses proves successful with other groups, we are persuaded that the psychoanalytic interview will provide a tool for the study of the "non-patient" better than any other now available. The use of this tool in literally hundreds of psychosocial projects where one wants specific information about groups who are not patients, is an exciting possibility.

Most apparent is the possible usefulness of such interviewing as a means of studying various groups within a given culture. For example, although the interests of the investigators were not related to nurses per se (this group having been chosen only because of its availability), the results suggest interesting hypotheses related to characteristics of successful nurses in our society.

In examining the interview material (corroborated by test data), one is struck by the paucity of evidence related to "mothering," "nurturing," "helping," "succorant" impulses or motivations. Rather, the total data emphasize the predominance of impulses related to the need to dominate, manipulate, control, rather than to those motivations ordinarily conceived as a major determinant in the choice of nursing as a career. Throughout the material there is also evidence of difficulties these nurses may have in relation to the problem of human intimacy, with the suggestion that their anxiety about it may have played a role in their career-choice. Although it is not known to what degree these nurses in a large metropolitan hospital are typical of nurses in general, some challenging hypotheses are presented for further investigation by those specifically interested in nursing education. A similar study of other professional or occupational groups would also be of great interest. The techniques have importance, too, in the study of such problems in different cultures. For example, in the already mentioned comparable study of twelve Norwegian nurses done by Hendin in Norway, the abundance of mothering, protective impulses on the part of the nurses was striking, but—and this is important to note—this also proved to be characteristic of Norwegian women in general.

This last point suggests that the use of psychoanalytic interviewing techniques has much wider application in the study of other cultures than merely the examination of particular occupational groups. In Hendin's Scandinavian work distinctive psychodynamic differences were apparent between Swedish and Norwegian nurses. As was noted in the introductory chapter, however, while the predominant psychological characteristics observed in Norwegian nurses differed from those of Swedish nurses, the patterns observed in both groups correlated well with those observed in Norwegians and Swedes who were psychiatric patients.

Psychoanalytic theory was built up from the study of patients, yet it predicates psychological postulates that are meant to apply to the "non-patient" as well. The fact that a "normal" psychoanalytic psychology has developed out of a study of the "abnormal" has been raised as an objection to many of the most common psychoanalytic concepts. The possibilities of checking among "non-patients" on the "universality," or at least the "frequency," of the psychoanalytic observations made with patients are self-evident. Even in the limited foregoing material, although this was not our focus, it is easy to observe many of the psychodynamic patterns seen daily with patients.

Discussion, Conclusions, Applications

Within psychoanalysis itself there has been criticism of theoretical formulations, such as the basic role given to difficulties in emotional communication by Harry Stack Sullivan or the innate destructiveness postulated by Melanie Klein, on the ground that these generalizations about "people" are based on the study of schizophrenic adults and schizophrenic children. Testing psychodynamic concepts with non-patients can help clarify such matters.

Obviously five interviews are not going to lead to the kind of information one gets in a psychoanalysis, and while one can get confirmatory evidence for certain characteristics, not finding them cannot eliminate the possibility that further investigation would do so. On the other hand, the analyst is often able to see in a few interviews things that it will take his patient years to learn. Certainly as much information was derived from the twelve "non-patients" in the present study as is derived from actual patients seen over a similar period of time.

One reason for the use of the somewhat awkward term "non-patient" stems from the fact that the subjects in this study turned out to have as much evidence of impairment in function as comparably seen patients in psychiatric practice.

There is no reason to believe that nurses are a more disturbed group than any other. As a group defined by society as normal and functioning relatively productively in their daily work, they undoubtedly reveal the personality strengths and weaknesses of a large majority of the general population who never come to the attention of any psychopathologist, either psychoanalyst, psychiatrist, or psychologist.

It is apparent that the distinction between patient and non-patient is not the same as that between sick and well. The discrepancy between how these individuals function and any textbook description of "healthy" or "ideal" adjustment is striking. The interesting question then arises as to what integrative forces permit individuals to function, often with purpose and adaptation, constructively and productively in spite of underlying difficulties. What integrative forces permit them to tolerate their own pathology without massive anxiety, regression, or disruption of equilibrium? And the answers to this question have primary importance for social as well as psychological research. It is somewhat disconcerting that in the present study the nurse whom the interviewer identified as one of the most disturbed girls was also described as "dramatic and engaging," while the "colorlessness" of one of the most normal of the group led the interviewer to speculate on how depressing it would be if this is what constitutes "normality."

What makes one individual with problems seek help while another does not? It is interesting to note, for example, that the nurses who were emotionally lifeless did not torture themselves over their inability to feel more—they were simply resigned to it in ways that private patients who come for help with these difficulties are not. Obviously a major factor is the girl's own expectations and aspirations for herself. The very procedure used in this study could profitably be further employed as a research tool in understanding what does or does not motivate people to seek psychiatric help, as well as in helping to understand what molds their expectations and aspirations.